INVESTIGATIVE RESEARCH

Theory and Practice

DEREK LAYDER

INVESTIGATIVE RESEARCH

Theory and Practice

SAGE

Los Angeles | London | New Delhi
Singapore | Washington DC | Melbourne

SAGE

Los Angeles | London | New Delhi
Singapore | Washington DC | Melbourne

SAGE Publications Ltd
1 Oliver's Yard
55 City Road
London EC1Y 1SP

SAGE Publications Inc.
2455 Teller Road
Thousand Oaks, California 91320

SAGE Publications India Pvt Ltd
B 1/I 1 Mohan Cooperative Industrial Area
Mathura Road
New Delhi 110 044

SAGE Publications Asia-Pacific Pte Ltd
3 Church Street
#10-04 Samsung Hub
Singapore 049483

Editor: Jai Seaman
Assistant editor: Alysha Owen
Production editor: Vanessa Harwood
Marketing manager: Susheel Gokarakonda
Cover design: Bhairvi Gudka
Typeset by: C&M Digitals (P) Ltd, Chennai, India
Printed in the UK

First edition published 2018

Library of Congress Control Number: 2017947310

British Library Cataloguing in Publication data

A catalogue record for this book is available from the British Library

ISBN 978-1-4462-8752-1
ISBN 978-1-4462-8753-8 (pbk)

CONTENTS

DETAILED CONTENTS

ABOUT THE AUTHOR

Derek Layder is Emeritus Professor of Sociology at the University of Leicester and Honorary Professor of Health and Life Sciences at De Montfort University. In 1974 he was appointed Lecturer in Sociology at the University of Leicester and in 1976 was awarded a doctorate by the London School of Economics. In 1995 he was promoted to Reader, then to Professor in 1997 and to Emeritus Professor from 2002. He has held several visiting academic positions and has also held honorary visiting appointments at The Australian National University (as a Humanities Research Fellow) and the University of Western Sydney (as Eminent Research Visitor). He taught in areas of social theory, social psychology, social research methods and the philosophy of social sciences. He has published numerous academic articles and 12 books. Among his books, in the area of the philosophy of social science, he is the author of *The Realist Image in Social Science* (1990); in social theory, he has written *Understanding Social Theory* (second edition, 2006), as well as *Modern Social Theory* (1997). On research strategies and methods, he has authored *New Strategies in Social Research* (1993), *Sociological Practice* (1998) and *Doing Excellent Small-Scale Research* (2013). He has also written on intimacy, emotion and self-identity, including *Emotion in Social Life* (2004), *Social & Personal Identity* (2004) and *Intimacy & Power* (2009).

INTRODUCTION

CHAPTER CONTENTS

WHAT IS INVESTIGATIVE RESEARCH?

Investigative research (IR) marries evidence-based explanations of social behaviour with distinctive strategies of data collection. It has been used with a wide range of topics and examples, including the emotional life of prisoners (Knight 2016), the professional practice of social workers (Houston 2015) and probation officers (Knight 2014), the adoption of information technology (Pruulmann-Vengerfeldt 2006), social trust and life insurance (Morris 2011), women's experience of egg freezing (Baldwin 2016) and gay sadomasochism (Chaline 2008), to mention but a few. IR searches out the influence of those parts of society that are frequently overlooked by other approaches. Its unique modelling and mapping of social processes enable IR to reach those parts of the social world other approaches cannot reach!

This book outlines the reasons why IR valuably adds to the existing armoury of research methods and approaches. Comparing IR with other approaches reveals it's comprehensive, inclusive model of social processes and its distinctive investigative strategies. Chapters 1–4 show how IR offers researchers an 'alternative' to existing approaches and a set of complementary practical skills and rules of thumb. Chapters 5–8 examine core aspects of the IR approach and discuss ways in which researchers may incorporate its principles in their own research projects.

The term 'investigative research' brings together different strands of work. In previous publications, I have referred to these strands in several different ways, but in fact they express a unified set of ideas. There are two main blocks of ideas that I have attempted to integrate here. The first concerns a 'research map' and its associated research methods and strategies (Layder 1993), further developed using terms such as 'adaptive theory', 'adaptive method', 'adaptive analysis' (Layder 1998, 2013). The other main tranche of ideas I have variously called 'the theory of social domains', 'domain theory', the 'domains model of social reality' or the 'domains framework' (Layder 1997, 2006). Given this array of terms, it seems tidier to group them together as 'investigative research' – or IR for short.

INVESTIGATION AS EXPLORATION

Does 'investigative research' have anything in common with investigative journalism or criminal investigation? There are indeed parallels, such as a central puzzle or incident which needs to be resolved or cleared up, a search for clues, the collection of evidence, the identification of key individuals (in the case of crime, perpetrator(s) and witnesses), and a chain of reasoning that ties these elements together and explains the initial puzzle or incident. However, IR has some unique characteristics:

- IR has a combined and integrated emphasis on research 'exploration', 'description' and 'explanation', based on their strong, mutually informative links.

This contrasts with approaches that view them as separate and 'stand-alone' activities with nothing to say or contribute to each other.

- IR has a structured, but flexible, starting point which is open to the influence of new ideas and to the potential revision of established views, assumptions and explanations – via adaptive responses to 'challenging' data and evidence.
- In IR, data samples are not fixed in advance or for the duration of a project. Changes in their composition often reflect subtle responses to emerging evidence and shifting analytical ideas.
- IR can be used to explain social behaviour in any empirical area. However, as with data samples, research problems are not rigidly 'determined' in advance. Rather, they are 'explored' theoretically and empirically during research. The exact contours of problems and their solutions depends on what research evidence reveals, and this cannot be prefigured, say, by the 'imposition' of a fully developed conceptual framework.

Investigative research is exploratory in character in the sense of being open to possible outcomes, regardless of the amount of previous research on the area or problem. During such exploration, a researcher must display a readiness to discover new angles on a phenomenon or problem, or to see them in a different light, or from alternative perspectives. This requires the use of the theoretical (analytical) imagination in combination with practical skills in the systematic collection of empirical evidence.

A GUIDE TO READING AND USING THIS BOOK

Chapter 1 stands somewhat apart from the other chapters. It focuses on crucially important, but much neglected, questions, such as: In what ways are practical issues – of research design, data collection and analysis – linked with general social processes and underlying features of social reality? How are models and maps of social reality crucial to the formulation of research problems and questions? Understanding these links is essential if social research is to produce cumulative, scientifically-based knowledge. Since such issues are scarcely mentioned – if at all – in most research methods texts, it is essential for researchers to be aware of their implications for research designs, strategies and data analysis.

Chapters 2, 3 and 4 emphasize the distinctive features of IR through comparisons with both 'competing' and complementary approaches. It must be noted that these chapters are not meant as introductions to, or full accounts of, alternate approaches. While the broadly inclusive nature of IR acknowledges the strengths of other approaches, it also departs from them in many other respects. Chapter 2 first outlines the core dimensions of research, which form the basis for comparisons and evaluations of different approaches. It then moves on to discuss selected aspects of survey methods, theory-testing approaches and three strands of qualitative research. They are assessed in terms of their potential use as complementing some central features of IR, particularly its qualitative core and its theory-generating objectives. The chapter concludes with some practical suggestions about how to incorporate elements of all these approaches into a more general context of IR.

In terms of the core dimensions of research, Chapter 3 focuses on selected aspects of case study research and mixed-methods approaches. The first part of the chapter focuses exclusively on Yin's (2009) version of case study research, since its sophisticated use of theory is not found in other versions and represents a very interesting contrast with IR's use of theory (see Chapter 6). The second part on mixed methods draws from a wider range of authors and examines the approach in a more general sense. The chapter concludes with advice about using aspects of these approaches to complement or supplement IR projects in relation to research design, data sampling, data collection and analysis. Chapter 4 concentrates on a comparison of IR with two versions of the 'grounded theory' approach. The chapter outlines the radically distinctive differences between grounded theory and IR. It concludes with examples of how coding and data analysis in IR involve very different assumptions and procedures.

Chapters 5, 6, 7 and 8 examine particular issues in IR and its practical application. Chapter 5 sets outs the main phases and cycles of the investigative approach. It describes the sorts of problems encountered during the unfolding of an IR project, and possible solutions. Chapter 6 deals with the use of theory in empirical research. It focuses on the types of theory most relevant to IR, and how they may be adapted to its aims, findings and conclusions. Chapter 7 spotlights empirical connections between social domains and networks, and examines related key issues. These include how to identify relevant data threads, dealing with problems arising in the analysis of different types of social setting, and dealing with the issue of causality. Chapter 8 discusses quality control in investigative research. The notions of validity and validation, in particular, are discussed as a continuous, ongoing feature of the investigative approach. Finally, I have included a glossary of investigative research terms.

I would like to thank those researchers who have used my work to inform and help organize their own studies. They have reassured me of the point and usefulness of domain theory and adaptive method, and without doubt their 'enthusiasm' for the ideas encouraged me to develop them here a little further. Victoria Knight has been particularly supportive and helpful over the past few years and her influence is reflected at many points in this book. I am grateful to Victoria and Thilo Boeck for inviting me to lead a discussion of my work at De Monfort University in 2012. This and a seminar at Aalborg University (at the invitation of Antje Gimmler and Poul Poder) have also influenced some of the ideas that appear in this book. Finally, I would like to thank Jai Seaman of SAGE, and two anonymous reviewers of an earlier form of the manuscript, for their useful suggestions.

1

RESEARCH MODELS, PROBLEMS AND QUESTIONS

CHAPTER CONTENTS

THE IMPORTANCE OF MODELS AND MAPS

Question: Why should researchers spend time examining 'underlying' models of social reality and the research maps endorsed by various approaches to research? Answer: First, all social investigation is influenced by such models and maps, thus, researchers should be aware of how they influence research practice and findings. Second, because, unfortunately, methods texts make little or no mention of these issues, researchers typically remain unaware of their influence and importance.

Consider, for example, a research project that aims to explain how and why prisoners deal with their emotions in the prison setting. It would be important for the researcher to work with a model and research map of the social world that represented *all the relevant dimensions* of the prison experience. However, if she or he was using a model that stressed only one dimension, say individual psychology, then research based on it would fall short. Similarly, if the only focus was on interpersonal relations, again, the result would be skewed and partial research findings. If the research emphasized only power and control in the prison regime, to the exclusion of other factors, then again, analysis would be lacking. Clearly, each model (or map) prioritizes different factors or dimensions of social life and considers them to be the most 'important' for an adequate account. However, the 'clarity' gained from such a concentrated focus is always at the price of overlooking the influence of equally important dimensions necessary for a comprehensive, fully inclusive explanation of social behaviour.

In sharp contrast, investigative research rests on a variegated, multidimensional model of the social world – the social domains framework. This, in conjunction with the 'adaptive' method, offers an integrated, inclusive platform, which allows researchers to access multiple viewpoints and dimensions. In so doing it makes available a wider range of pertinent empirical data and theoretical resources to support a robust and comprehensive understanding of social behaviour – in the above example, of emotional life in prison (see Knight 2016; Knight and Layder 2016).

In short, researchers need models and maps which provide inclusive overviews of the research area, problem or topic. A map that only covers 'selected' areas or a model that omits or conceals significant parts of the social world will be lacking in important respects. This chapter traces the development of IR's *entangled domains* model of social reality as an alternative to the one-dimensional models in regular research use. As a necessary prelude to this we must probe a little deeper into the reasons why models and maps of social reality have important consequences for research practice and research methods. A major reason in this regard is the persistence of a 'false' gap between social theory and social research methods.

CLOSING GAPS IN KNOWLEDGE

For entirely different reasons, both research methods experts and general social theorists have failed to grasp the important influences that underlying models of social reality have on research methods and research findings. General social theorists (for example, Habermas, Foucault, Giddens) have interesting and significant things to say about the nature of social reality. Typically, however, they do not concern themselves with methods and strategies of data collection. An unfortunate consequence is that they ignore the practical implications that 'models of social reality' have on empirical social research. On the other hand, methods 'experts' and methods texts concentrate on research methods as technical instruments of data collection and thus, again, do not acknowledge the relevance and influence of models of reality.

In this state of affairs, important links between empirical social research, general theory and models of social reality 'disappear' into the 'false' gap between theory and methods, created by 'methods' specialists and 'theory' specialists. True enough, researchers sometimes use bits and pieces of theory to 'decorate' or add gravitas to their research findings but, like methods texts, they fail to recognize the importance and relevance of links between models of reality, theory and evidence. On the other hand, theorists (and theory texts) often assume that 'theory' and 'methods' are quite separate areas of expertise and fail to register or understand their mutual influences. Some theoretical purists display no interest whatsoever in applying abstract concepts and ideas to practical data-gathering research projects. The result is that theorists and researchers routinely ignore, or 'talk past' each other. Most damagingly, the absence of discussion about the connections between models of reality, general social theory and research methods erodes the scientific credibility of social research. It seems that theorists and researchers are happy to shun engagement with one another. Thus, they fail to nurture possible advancements in knowledge that might ensue. Investigative research works towards overcoming this gap in an effort to stimulate properly *cumulative* knowledge via the synergy between different strands of analysis.

INFLUENTIAL MODELS OF SOCIAL REALITY

Crucially, models of social reality limit or expand the 'legitimate' range of investigative problems, as illustrated in the earlier example of researching emotion in prison life. Built into such models are implicit attempts to resolve, ignore or otherwise 'get around' the 'agency–structure' problem that is central to social analysis (Giddens 1984; Archer 1995). In this sense, models of social reality are blueprints that implicitly attempt to reconcile the effects of human action (agency) on social life (structure or organization) and vice versa. Such models contain concealed answers to questions such as: Are the consequences and effects of social activity (agency) on social organization long-term, or only fleeting? Do they produce stable patterns in the social world? Is human activity (agency) shaped by existing social expectations, habits, routines and ideology, or does it shape such phenomena? This book is primarily about practical matters of research and so I have kept the following discussion as brief and as condensed as possible. It sketches the main responses to the agency–structure problem (for more detail see Layder 2006), while outlining and revealing the models of social reality that underpin and inform these responses. Such models of reality implicitly 'map' areas of social reality and mark them out as legitimate research subjects or targets which are 'available' for empirical investigation.

1 Structures determine agency

Some theorists explain social behaviour (agency) as an effect of structural or systemic features of society (Parsons 1951). In this view, society is an overarching social 'system' or 'structure' which in large measure shapes human action (behaviour and agency), leaving little or no 'creative' role for individual (or collective) agents. People are regarded mainly as ciphers or playthings of greater social forces, a view which trivializes their creative and 'causal' contributions.

2 All is human agency: rejecting structures and systems

Many authors reject the very existence of structures or systems, believing they are 'inventions' of social scientists or theorists. Instead, social institutions – and the wider 'macro order' – are simply products of the observable behaviour of people. There are variants of this view. Blumer (1969), for instance, prefers to talk about 'joint action', Schutz (1972) speaks of the 'intersubjective world', Collins (2005) about 'interaction ritual chains', Becker (1970) about 'people doing things together', Garfinkel (1967) and Hilbert (1990) focus on 'local practices'. In sum, this position (and the model of social reality it supports) asserts that collective (or structural) phenomena are nothing more than the aggregate effects of micro encounters.

3 'False dualism': refusing to engage

Some authors reject both agency and structure as a false and static 'dualism'. Instead they speak of ever-changing social flows and forces, such as 'actor-networks', 'mobilities', 'liquidities', 'discourses', 'powers and practices' or 'rhizomatic flows'. For instance, Elias's concept of 'figurations' (networks of interdependency relations) has been hailed as a way of 'circumventing the agency–structure problem' (Dunning and Hughes 2013). Unfortunately, the agency–structure problem needs to be resolved, not ignored by refusing to engage with it! It isn't enough to claim that dualisms (including macro and micro) are false. The problem of how society and social processes are simultaneously produced and reproduced via ongoing activities and practices must be explained, not explained away, by circumvention.

4 Giddens' duality of structure

Giddens (1984) acknowledges the importance of the agency–structure (and macro–micro) problems, but at the same time insists that they do not refer to separate and opposed aspects of society. He thus replaces the 'dualism' of 'agency and structure' with what he calls the 'duality of structure', which, unfortunately, collapses them together, leaving their mutual influences unexplained. For Giddens, structures only exist in action as actor's memory traces, motivations and reasons. As a consequence, any partly independent effects of structures (and systems) are reduced to aspects of agency. Giddens fails to entertain the possibility that agency and structure are *different and connected* (through interdependence), rather than separate and opposed. He does not envisage the possibility that their different properties might coexist while still being relatively autonomous (for more detail see Layder 1997, 2006).

5 Analytical dualism: agency and structure upheld

As an alternative to the above approaches, analytical dualism insists that the distinct properties of agency and structure cannot be reduced or dissolved into each other. For analytical dualists, agency and structure causally influence each other in various ways (Berger and Luckmann 1967; Habermas 1986, 1988; Archer 1995). However, the basic drawback of analytical dualism as a model is that it is not subtle enough to capture the full complexity of social reality.

6 Entangled social domains: researching social complexity

Investigative research is underpinned by a nuanced and complex model of social reality which reflects the ontological variegation of modern society. The theory of domains is based on four principal interrelated social processes: 'psychobiography', 'situated activity', 'social settings' and 'contextual resources', each of which has its own properties and dimensions of power, time and space (Layder 1997).

SHOULD MODELS BE ELIMINATIVE OR INTEGRATIVE?

Researchers must ask: Which model of social reality best serves social research? Which more accurately depicts and explains the complexity of modern society? Which model raises the most pertinent questions about social processes? What empirical research questions are 'closed-off' or 'eliminated' by particular models? Which research problems are endorsed and legitimized by particular models?

Models 1–5 are reductive in so far as they are based on the 'elimination' of those aspects of social reality deemed to be false, illusory or redundant. In models 3 and 4 the social terrain is reduced to 'unifying' (synthetic) principles – 'duality of structure', 'local practices', 'figurations', 'actor-networks', 'discourses'. As a result, social reality is simplified. The effects of human psychology and individual differences are eliminated from consideration, while the partly separate effects of situated activity, social settings and contexts are simply ignored. Overall, models 1–5 artificially limit research interest to one or at best two dimensions of social reality. For empirical research, these 'eliminated dimensions' pose an important problem since they represent important sites and sources of evidence, essential for the study of social behaviour.

The IR model of entangled domains (model 6) restores these 'eliminated' dimensions by integrating complementary aspects of social reality. In this sense, the domains framework acts as a 'holding platform' which both restores missing domains and encourages constructive dialogue between sometimes radically different standpoints and assumptions. It offers a model of social reality founded on a balanced synthesis of subjective, inter-subjective and objective aspects of social life and thus endorses a wide-ranging, inclusive research agenda.

ENTANGLED DOMAINS AND RESEARCH

Social domains are intertwined through networks of power relations, while social behaviour is formed from the concerted influence of all the domains. In particular circumstances, however, a focus on one or two domains may point to a causal account of social behaviour, while other circumstances might require attention to two or three. In this sense, 'selective focusing' allows researchers to concentrate on one or two domains while acknowledging the (simultaneous) 'background' influence of others. Thus, it resolves the practical problem of dealing with too many factors at the same time and particularly affects smaller projects with limited budgets.

For the investigative researcher, the domains model can yield provisional clues as to which domains are most causally relevant to the project and research problem at hand. However, a full and detailed causal account can only be revealed in the light of ongoing data collection and analysis. Importantly, the variegated domains model *brings to life* precisely those unfolding social processes that are eliminated, and thus suppressed by, vertical and flat models alike. The domains of 'psychobiography', 'situated activity', 'social settings' and 'contextual resources' are interlinked but partly autonomous social processes unfolding over different time frames.

RESTORING LOST DOMAINS: INVESTIGATIVE RESEARCH PROBLEMS AND QUESTIONS

Psychobiography

Psychobiography traces personal psychological changes as they intertwine with, and influence, social relations and involvements throughout an individual's life.

Research areas and questions opened up by this domain include:

- Psychobiography places the research focus on the development of personal and social identity, motives, emotions, personal 'style', and so on, over the course of individual life 'careers'. It traces subjective changes caused by experiences such as friendships, romantic and/or sexual partnerships, and so on, in relation to different settings (work, family, leisure, crime). The personal meanings and emotional impact of these vary over time, and shape individuals' motives, feelings and social responses.
- A psychobiographical focus reveals whether individuals feel fulfilled, committed or entrapped by work, family or personal relationships, and how they affect subsequent experiences – of work or the 'fate' of marriages, sexual partnerships or friendships.
- Research might focus on the responses of individuals to authority and control in the workplace (such as workers with line managers) or how partners deal with interpersonal control in intimate relationships.
- Research problems and questions might centre on the experience of simultaneous 'mini-careers', which can create problems of coping and tests of resilience. For instance, juggling the effects of unemployment or illness, or infidelity on a marriage or partnership, may lead to insecurity, fear, or loss of self-confidence or self-esteem.
- Do ambitions, desires and aspirations lead to selfish and greedy motives or to more empathetic and altruistic ones?

Subjective power and psychobiographical time

Subjective power is an important aspect of psychobiography. It shapes personal desires hopes and objectives – particularly the capacity for interpersonal control (which can be 'benign' or 'manipulative'; Layder 2004) and the personal capacity to change one's social circumstances. Many research models (of social reality) dismiss the importance of the subjective dimension of power and insist that it is an exclusively social property or force. Psychobiography also has its own properties of temporality. While it is true that self–identity retains common features over time, it is important not to think of it as a fixed essence. A psychobiographical focus points to its unfolding and developmental character over the individual lifespan.

Opening up research problems and questions

Psychobiography spotlights a person's psychological 'depth', its impact on the social world, and vice versa, as it unfolds over time and space. Psychobiography points to the tensions between the desire for social inclusion (relatedness) and the opposing desire for independence, and the right to say no to social involvement. Recognizing psychobiography as a domain in its own right makes it possible to pose research questions about the links between lived (social) experiences and personal emotional responses. With many models of social reality human subjectivity 'disappears' into a black hole of 'social interaction' or 'social practices', or 'social networks'. For instance, flat network models overstress 'lateral connections' and information flows, neglecting human feelings, desires and the importance of the personal 'inner life'. The domains framework reinstates the importance of this inner life. In fact, without recognizing the partly autonomous influence of psychobiography it would be impossible to properly study or understand certain questions and problems – for example, physical or mental illness, drug taking, criminality or intimacy.

Of course, the psychobiographical domain does not exist or operate entirely free from the influence of social constraints. Indeed, understanding the role of social constraints is central to adequate explanations of social behaviour. Unfortunately, however, many social researchers exaggerate the influence of social forces and thereby gloss-over the effects of individual differences and powers. The domains model suggests that social behaviour stems from the reciprocal, confluent influences of psychobiographies, situated activities, social settings and contextual resources – and their different types of power.

The domain of situated activity

Situated activity focuses on the ways in which people influence one another as they connect through social interaction or 'encounters' (face-to-face, or via electronic means such as phones, tablets, lap-tops, email, Facebook, Twitter, and so on).

Examples of research problems, topics and questions

- Some encounters are fleeting such as on the street, with members of the public (strangers), or for the duration of journey (in adjacent seats on planes, buses and trains). Others are repeated over variable periods of time, such as those with work colleagues, friends or family. Research might examine whether such characteristics affect the quality of the activities (encounters) and if they achieve what they set out to achieve.
- How are the self-identities (psychobiographies) of participants influenced by encounters? What situational meanings, rules and roles are created and shared? What effects do social settings (prisons, airports, hospitals, care homes, factories, offices, bedrooms, sports events) have on encounters and situated activities? Does the 'formality' of the setting make a difference?
- Research might examine, for example, how prisoners get on (or fail to) with fellow prisoners, cell-mates, prison officers, probation staff, and so on. The study might reveal shared advice on coping with the stresses of prison life, and feelings of alienation and boredom.
- Important for research would be *the purpose* of encounters, such as support, gossip, information, criticism, competition or threats. Asking for loving gestures in intimate relationships or for 'more emotional space' are linked with the use of benign control (as in concern for an elderly parent or a child) or with the use of more selfish, manipulative control (as in abuse, bullying, kidnapping or paedophilia).
- Central to such topics would be the study of talk – the ways in which participants take turns at speaking, or open and close conversations. Who is included (or excluded) from conversations and why are also central issues. Which conversational styles are used – 'direct' or 'indirect'?

Situational power and time frames

A person may be powerful in one situation (or in relation to one issue), but not so in others, or in other contexts. A CEO of a multinational company might be decisive and controlling at work, but meek and deferential at home or in personal relationships. Conversely, someone who has low formal status may be heroic in an emergency. There is a subtle interaction between subjective, situational, settings and contextual factors and influences. Situated activity has an evanescent quality to it. Some encounters are brief and one-off, as with strangers on streets or in car parks, trains or aircraft. Others are regularly repeated, as between friends, work colleagues or within family networks.

Although all these elements of situated activity are important in their own right, they are shaped to a greater or lesser extent by the action of other domains, such as psychobiography (as reflected in the expression of the emotional needs of the self via personal style), the type of setting in which they occur, and the wider social backdrop of contextual resources (such as class, age, gender, ethnicity).

Opening up research questions

Situated activity filters and conditions the influences of other domains, and is the site of the 'interaction order' (Goffman 1983). Unfortunately, some researchers (influenced by model 2), have exaggerated the importance of situated activity and focus exclusively on it (Blumer 1969; Becker 1970). Without doubt, situational and emergent elements are crucially important, but they do not operate in isolation – they develop out of the interlinked influences of other entangled domains. Conversations, for example, cannot be accounted for entirely in terms of 'openings' and 'closings' or 'turn-taking' (Malone 1997). Clearly, extra-situational influences of psychobiography (personal power and style), social settings and wider contextual resources play crucially formative roles.

In stark contrast, other models completely suppress the causal and explanatory importance of situated activity and the role of the 'interaction order'. Giddens' 'structuration' model (1987) does this by dissolving the effects of the interaction order into the institutional order via the 'duality of structure'. Other models ignore the importance of situated activity altogether by focusing entirely on networks and interdependencies. In such cases, research is deprived not only of the analysis of emergent, shared meaning, but also of the effects of individual psychobiographies. Survey and experimental researchers typically either 'bracket-out' altogether the inter-subjective world – or the experiential core of social life – or reduce everyday social behaviour to the effects of researcher-defined, quantitative variables. As a consequence, a vast range of everyday behaviour (in coffee bars, clubs, courtrooms, restaurants, bedrooms, track-meets (Goffman 1967) is either explained in an overly simple manner or by-passed altogether as an area of research interest.

The domain of social setting(s)

With social settings the research spotlight is on the 'already established' character of different types of social settings – family networks, business networks, organizations, hospitals, banks, cafés, fast-food restaurants. The social organization of settings mediates and conditions the concerted influences of situated activity, psychobiography and contextual resources in shaping and moulding social behaviour.

Examples of research problems, topics and questions

- The social organization of factories, hospitals, families, gangs, schools, universities, crèches, religious groups or sects varies considerably. Some are quite formal while others are informally organized. In some settings, power and authority are arranged vertically and hierarchically, while in others they are horizontal/lateral or even 'situational'. In what ways do these differences influence activity? What secures attachment or commitment to settings?
- What is the experience of participants? Are employees alienated from or happy with their work environments and conditions? How do the perceptions and experiences of participants and/or customers in large, impersonal organizations (bureaucracies) compare with those in smaller, 'personalized' settings (like local cafés and small businesses)? What range of emotional expression is expected of doctors, flight attendants or probation officers in their respective work settings?
- How does the 'external', cultural and economic context impinge on settings, as measured by the influence of societal values, fashion, media, gender, ethnicity, class?

Settings, positional power and time frames

In many settings, power is associated with career systems in which the achievement of formal positions of authority or expertise are rewarded by rises in income and status. In other settings (like gangs or families), positions and statuses are more informally defined and backed up by less predictable sanctions (such as avoidance, exclusion or violence). Power and control may be benign (as in some forms of intimacy) or they may be manipulative and exploitative (as in crime, sexual harassment, bullying and abuse). As far as temporality is concerned, settings have 'organizational' histories of their own and operate according to their own, sometimes very different, rhythms of time.

Opening up research possibilities

'Social settings' are the immediate arenas in which everyday situated activity takes place and thus, the two are tightly bound together. Of course, in one sense social settings only exist in virtue of the actions of people, but they also have a 'reproduced', or 'already established' character which ensures their continuance beyond specific activities and specific people. In this sense, the habitual actions of previous participants (in some cases many generations of them) are sedimented over time and space, and are reflected in current practices, rules, positional powers and expectations.

Individuals move between multiple settings *in their daily round,* as well as *over their whole life-careers.* They range from the formality of organizations (hospitals, universities, fast-food restaurants) to rather amorphous groupings and networks, such as gangs, friendships and street life/culture.

'Flat' models of social reality, in particular, do not acknowledge social settings as partly independent domains and instead 'reduce' them to the analysis of networks and/or connections. Of course, networks (or 'relational interdependencies') are important for social analysis and research. They clearly are part of, and 'run through', domain processes and interlinked relations of power. However, at the same time, networks and figurations are importantly conditioned and influenced by these same domain processes. Indeed, in Chapter 7, I deal with some of the ways in which the investigative approach can be used to research connections between networks and social domains. Unfortunately, however, eliminative and reductive models exclude the importance of domains, which in fact are crucial to a rounded understanding of networks and social behaviour. Only a multidimensional model can gain access to the complexity of social processes by tapping into other dimensions of social reality.

The domain of contextual resources

In the domain of contextual resources, the research focus is on the ways in which social behaviour is shaped and influenced by cultural values, expectations and institutions, media, class, income and life chances, gender, ethnicity, politics, neighbourhood and region.

Examples of research problems, topics and questions

- Research might focus on the ways in which political, economic, religious and ethnic factors influence social behaviour. To what extent are drug taking, smoking and alcohol consumption shaped by factors such as class, gender, age, region and ethnicity?
- How do newspapers, magazines, films, music and websites, blogs, and so on, shape social attitudes, values, fashions and behaviour?
- Why are certain groups discriminated against, bullied or harassed? Do inequalities of power and economic circumstances influence such behaviour? How do people deal with the fear of gang violence, paramilitary violence or terrorism?

Such problems and questions reflect the tight connections between wider contextual (social systemic) factors and individual psychobiographies, as they are channelled via situated activities and a range of social settings (terrorist organizations, gangs, family networks).

Systemic (or structural) power and historical time

Systemic power refers to power that derives from a group's position in the wider macro organization of society – an important element of contextual resources. Inequalities of power between groups are based on the unequal distributions of resources. The domain of contextual resources is linked with the largest sense of the passing of time, marking out epochal changes in society, as well as transitions between societal types, such as that between feudal society and capitalist society.

Opening up research possibilities

'Macro' or society-wide influences stray beyond the boundaries of particular fields of activity and are marked by inequalities of power and life chances. Social status, power, authority, money, property and possessions are distributed between groups in the form of economic and cultural asymmetries. Such forms of inequality profoundly affect people's life chances and experiences, and, as a consequence, their feelings, values and aspirations. Core political and economic institutions (and their supporting ideologies) also influence and shape behaviour. In this sense, contextual resources significantly mould individual psychobiographies and everyday situated activities. In the longer term, forms of activity feed into the construction of new elements of the macro order. Many models of social reality do not recognize the existence of a macro order (and hence of contextual resources) and thus significant (and legitimate) research problems and questions are ruled out. The domains framework reinstates the variegation and complexity of social reality, thus expanding research possibilities and the growth of genuinely cumulative knowledge.

RESEARCH PROBLEMS, TOPICS AND QUESTIONS

As the forgoing discussion has indicated, models and maps of social reality can be used to guide and direct research either by opening up or expanding (as with the domains model) or by shutting down or restricting the range and nature of research 'problems' and 'questions' (as with models 1–5). In essence, models of social reality simultaneously draw *attention to* certain areas, topics and problems and *away from* others. Often these effects remain implicit and unacknowledged. As a result, their influences on what can or should be researched, what problems posed, what questions asked, remain undisclosed, hidden and dormant. With investigative research, such links are explicitly discussed and openly acknowledged. Thus, we have the following sequence:

Research problems flow directly from the domains model – which directs research towards certain empirical areas and targets data (evidence facts and information) that best document domain processes. By contrast,

Research questions point to the data or evidence that are most pertinent to the solution of research problems and explanations of social behaviour.

Core research questions are the key questions on which a research project is centred, and around which it coheres. Core questions are, in fact, a fusion of *problem questions* and *topic questions*, which complement each other, but are based on rather different assumptions and principles.

Problem questions tend to be general (having implications beyond the current project), as well as more conceptual and abstract. An example would be: How do the situated activities of drug users impact on their self-identities or psychobiographies?

Topic questions are typically more specific (local to the project), concrete and empirical. For example: What is the frequency of drug use in an occupational group?

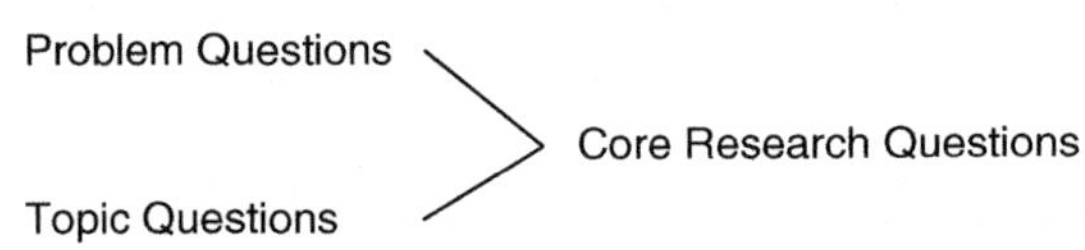

The decisive role of problem questions

In IR, by far the most important role in the selection of the core research questions for a particular project is played by 'problem' questions. So, although core questions are a blend of problem and topic questions, problem questions have greater influence on the overall research agenda, including the construction of research designs and research proposals (see Layder 2013). In a more immediate sense, problem questions shape and limit topic questions. Topic questions are about local empirical facts and information, including who or what to include in data samples. Topic questions involve 'how many?', 'where?' and 'when?' questions, for example, in relation to drug taking, mental illness, work careers or intimate relationships. In IR, topic questions are filtered through relevant problem questions for several reasons:

- To shape and focus them on the most pertinent evidence, that is, data that are most likely to be decisive in either supporting or disconfirming research findings and to validate research conclusions (including the reasoning and arguments on which they are based).
- Constant filtering and conditioning of topic questions by a problem focus has the effect of limiting the number of topic questions generated by the researcher, thus keeping them to 'manageable' proportions as well as focused on the core problem.
- Filtering also helps researchers to make decisions about when to stop gathering data. Asking whether a topic question can contribute to the problem focus helps in answering research questions such as: 'Have I got enough evidence?' 'Have I got enough data to support my core (and satellite) concepts?' 'When should I stop ... topping-up my sample, ... interviewing, ... observing, ... surveying?'

ADAPTIVE METHOD AND THEORY

Structured exploration and flexible design

The domains model offers an image of social reality and a research template which make it easier to define initial research problems and to set the empirical parameters of core research questions. Importantly, it helps to formulate an initial 'conceptual scaffold', that is, the basis for the explanation of social behaviour under investigation. However, this structured starting point is never frozen into the design to become a fixed and permanent feature of the research, which 'determines' the outcome. Neither is this structure treated as 'a hypothesis' that the research sets out to prove either true or false. Rather, it functions as a structured starting point to get the project underway. From then onwards the research follows an exploratory and investigative trajectory. Incoming data is filtered and analysed, forcing the initial assumptions to adapt to what data reveal.

For example, a researcher might investigate the extent to which individual psychobiographies influence drug taking or alcohol habits in social settings such as schools, universities or workplaces. Alternatively, a project might focus on whether particular occupational settings give rise to experiences of oppression, discrimination or status enhancement. The domains model furnishes a general and provisional overview of the range of social phenomena and processes that will be relevant. Thus, the researcher has a structured launching point – a combination of domain concepts and relevant 'orienting concepts' (from existing theory about the area), which guide and direct data collection and analysis. Once begun, however, data collection and analysis filters, and sometimes challenges initial theory and concepts. How, and to what extent, the initial orienting scaffold of concepts will 'evolve' or transform in line with ongoing data collection will vary according to circumstances, but it will not remain unchanged.

At the start, the researcher has no firm convictions about the extent of the adaptive responses that may be required. This depends on what turns up during data collection, the gaps in knowledge that are revealed, and the extent to which analytical ideas transmute or transform during the course of the project.

The exploratory nature of the investigative approach favours broad-ranging strategies. In the research methods literature, 'exploratory' research refers to new or relatively unexplored areas about which there is little existing research knowledge. In this sense, it is often the case that the main objective of 'exploratory research' is theory-generation (perhaps with the longer-term aim of theory-testing in mind). With IR, however, while theory-generation (or theory development) remains central, the idea of theory-testing is not completely divorced from it, and so there is no rigid distinction between theory-testing and theory-generating.

In IR, 'exploratory' refers to the analytical orientation of the project irrespective of the extent to which the area or problem has already been researched, and/or the existing stock of theory and concepts. In this sense, exploration signals a commitment to opening-up the analysis to the principle of 'explanatory revisability'. Thus, investigative research explores analytical and explanatory possibilities as they are informed by incoming empirical data or evidence. A central focus of 'exploration' is on the interweaving links between agency–structure and macro–micro features of social life or, expressed differently, the links between the 'life-world' and 'system' (Habermas 1986, 1988) elements of social life. Examining the empirical world through the background lens of the domains perspective enables researchers to scrutinize interconnected areas of social reality.

The question of causality is essential to a scientific approach and is closely aligned with the problem of how social domains interrelate in specific empirical instances. Causality is concerned with the question of how one phenomenon, set of events or occurrences gives rise to others. It seeks answers to questions about 'why' something occurs, the reasons for its existence, and 'how' it appears – its form and content. The domains model allows researchers to reach a provisional understanding about causal processes with respect to the main research problem. For example, a research project might explore how gender, class, ethnicity or age (contextual resources) influence intimate communication or non-verbal gestures? Which domains are significant? Is intimacy best understood in relation to individual psychobiographies, situated activities or types of setting? It cannot be assumed prior to empirical investigation that any particular domain (or domains) is/are the most causally relevant. Such questions can only be resolved by reference to actual empirical research data and the researcher's openness to possible explanations and influences.

Clearly, with its exploratory nature, its revisable conceptual scaffold and research design, IR can generate a broad range of possible research outcomes. However, most outcomes fit somewhere between two extremes. On the one hand, some elements of 'testing' are relevant, even integral to particular projects. As I have said, as a general rule investigative research does not aim to test relationships between two or more variables (see Chapters 2 and 3). Rather, it sets out to explore a problem-focus by assessing possible explanations of how domains causally influence social behaviour. This encourages researchers working from structured designs to produce creative, innovative outcomes, as, for example, when new or unexplained data necessitate the modification, extension or elaboration of existing concepts. In this sense, the approach's openness to emergent possibilities makes it likely that at least some 'discovery' or 'addition' will occur in the form of challenging data or innovative conceptual analysis.

At the other end of the spectrum, adaptive responses require changes in the initial analytical scaffold. An original orienting concept (or cluster of concepts) may be 'modified' out of all recognition. But in an important sense, adaptive responses can only be 'measured' in relation to their deviation from the initial orienting concepts and assumptions. So although innovative, there remain some links with extant knowledge.

Perhaps the most productive outcome for investigative research involves an interweaving combination of modification (elaboration) and generation of knowledge, concepts and findings in the same project. Such a 'mixed outcome' adds to social scientific knowledge as a cumulative enterprise in two ways. First, it confirms – or at least gives strong support to – some aspects of an existing corpus of knowledge, while simultaneously critiquing, elaborating and extending it. Second, it contributes to knowledge accumulation through the emergence of innovative ideas, concepts and theory. In this sense, investigative research expands current boundaries of knowledge by providing new perspectives, concepts and/or analytical assumptions (see Chapter 6).

HAVING A SOLID BACK-STORY: TOP SOIL OR TAPROOTS?

This chapter has examined the links between models of social reality (society and social life) and how they influence research problems, questions, methods and strategies. The IR 'take' on these issues is that social research should be firmly anchored by a solid 'back-story'. Typically, methods textbooks simply supply 'lists' of methods that may be used to answer practical and technical questions concerning data collection or analysis. Extremely rarely do they discuss deeper questions (about the nature of social reality) because they assume that this would unnecessarily complicate what are, 'in fact', straightforward practical or technical issues and problems.

But these are precisely the sorts of questions that the IR approach encourages researchers to ask. Having a solid back-story, in this sense, ensures that empirical research is anchored in something more than the loose 'top-soil' of practical and technical adequacy. The objective should be to establish tap-root foundations for robust, cumulative knowledge. In this respect, research must confront and engage with – rather than avoid or 'circumvent' – significant questions lying beneath the surface. What does social reality consist of? What does it look like? How do people create and reproduce social life and social reality? How do domain processes operate in local circumstances? IR raises such empirical and analytical questions, and thus demands a blend of evidence and theoretical explanation.

SUMMARY OF KEY FEATURES OF INVESTIGATIVE RESEARCH

Research proposals and design

IR encourages and enables researchers to display an awareness of deep background issues in a relatively easy and accessible manner. Because of its fusion of the domains model with a specific empirical topic and data gathering project, IR 'pushes' researchers into more complex patterns of thought and analysis. In so doing it addresses early on the problem of research proposals often appearing to be hastily stitched together and lacking substance or analytical penetration.

Scientific basis

Investigative research is committed to scientific method and procedure, and thus it is not limited to describing research subjects/participants' 'worlds' or interpretations of their 'concerns' (Glaser 2001) or their 'accounts' of what they are doing (Charmaz 2012). Of course, these are all very important and have their place, *but they should not be the sole basis of research* – its methods or findings. Related to this, IR endorses a central role for qualitative data without rejecting the complementary contributions that quantitative data (and analysis) might make in particular circumstances. Importantly, qualitative data and analysis should never be regarded as 'subordinate to' quantitative data and method.

Unlike 'mixed methods', IR's 'multi-strategy' approach is not rooted in the philosophy of pragmatism, which rejects notions of truth and objectivity. Science is founded on theory and evidence-based truth claims, and thus, while for IR there are no final objective truths, there are certainly 'more limited' truth claims based on a moderate (rather than extreme) notion of objectivism. Science, as Searle (1998) points out, maintains an epistemic objectivity of method, even while investigating ontologically subjective subject matter. In this sense, scientific method can be used to study consciousness or 'qualia' or qualitative states (Searle 1998). For IR, these same considerations apply to the study of social life and to social research. As social scientists, we can study individual subjectivity, situated meaning and action, and deploy qualitative data and method, objectively and scientifically. The scientific basis of IR is reflected in its two-tier research focus – a general 'domains' model harnessed to a specific data-gathering project which allows access to a wide range of ontological subject matter (subjective, inter-subjective and systemic/objective), while maintaining an epistemic objectivity of method.

The importance of theory for science

Integral to science is the notion of theory-based explanations of empirical data or evidence. This is central to IR's blending of theory-testing and theory-generating research strategies. It also underlines an important role for 'general' or 'formal' theory and concepts but only in so far as they serve the aims of empirical research, and are themselves strongly anchored in empirical data.

Broader range of concepts

With its access to 'eliminated' realms of social reality (ontology), and its integrative use of a wide spectrum of forms of knowledge (epistemology), IR researchers deal with a much broader range of concepts, including 'system', 'behavioural' and 'bridging' types. This contrasts markedly with many qualitative approaches, including 'grounded theory', which are limited to 'behavioural' or 'action' concepts, formed around 'participant's concerns' (Glaser 2001), or Charmaz's (2008) concepts of 'doing' (see Chapter 4).

Enhanced validity

Triangulation – understanding data from several different vantage points (theory, methods, data and researchers) – has become an essential aspect of research more generally, since it is aimed at strengthening the verification and validation of data and research findings. The 'domains' model adds an extra dimension to triangulation by enabling researchers to consider data from different domain standpoints and, in so doing, increase the analytical relevance of particular research sites and data sources.

Research problems and questions

IR is problem-driven in relation to the construction of research questions. In practical terms, this helps researchers to shape and hone research questions in order to get them as sharp and focused as possible. Second, this in turn aids targeted data selection – by placing excess data to one side and keeping a keener eye on analytically more important, problem-focused data. Third, as a consequence, these make for easier management and storage of data. Fourth, the danger of researcher confusion resulting from juggling with too much data is significantly reduced. Fifth, the problem-led approach to constructing research questions helps address the problem of when to stop data-gathering or sampling, or deciding when you have enough data (to support concepts or explanations).

Selective focusing

In a single project it is practically, financially, analytically and mentally impossible to fully concentrate on all domain influences. The principle of 'selective focusing' allows researchers to concentrate intensively on two or three domain influences while 'bearing in the mind' the contributory influences of the others. Selective focusing also naturally leads researchers into some provisional thinking about causality and causal processes. Again, the domains model can help point to possible causal influences while the adaptive method allows researchers to focus in on targeted empirical data.

Accessing social reality and inter-disciplinary dialogue

Finally, a decisive advantage of IR is that it offers platforms which facilitate communication across competing and complementary discourses. IR cuts across many disciplinary boundaries, including sociology, anthropology, psychiatry, psychology, philosophy, economics, criminology, politics, macro analysis and micro analysis, among others. Based on integrative principles – the domains model plus adaptive method plus local data gathering research – allows IR to establish meaningful dialogue with any discipline that might make a positive contribution. But the route by which this is attained is principled and systematic and based on genuinely open debate. Second, by offering a multidimensional view of social reality, IR allows researchers the kind of access to domains (realms, areas or regions of reality) that is not possible via other approaches, alternative mappings of social reality and conceptions of research strategy.

2

DIMENSIONS, QUANTITY AND QUALITY

CHAPTER CONTENTS

This chapter compares IR with other approaches, with a view to helping researchers enhance the quality of their own projects. While I am generally concerned to stress the overall usefulness of IR, I do not claim that it is the solution to all problems or suits all purposes, but rather that its strengths lie in certain directions. Ultimately, the decision to use IR will depend on what the researcher wants for, and from, her or his project. However, by emphasizing IR's distinctive characteristics and potential advantages, I hope it will be easier to judge whether or not, and in what respects, it suits particular research purposes. This chapter compares IR with survey research, theory-testing research, and three qualitative strands of inquiry with the intention of helping researchers strengthen their own projects. I attempt to do this in two main ways. First, by showing how IR provides 'added extras' not contained in other approaches, and second, by encouraging researchers to draw on elements from these other approaches, if they add value to their own projects.

The details of what is involved are contained in the relevant sections, and also at the end of the chapter where research advice is offered in the form of questions for researchers to ask about their own research projects. The discussions (of other approaches) are not meant to be rounded expositions or 'introductions', nor are they meant to be exhaustive critiques. Rather, they concentrate only on selected factors – those that help to position IR in relation to them. However, before embarking on actual comparisons, I first outline some key dimensions of research. I hope this will make the discussion sharper and more meaningful. It will also shed light on the discussions in Chapters 3 and 4. Hopefully, examining and assessing the implications of these dimensions will also make it easier for researchers to decide which are most relevant to their own projects.

SOME BASIC DIMENSIONS OF RESEARCH

Use and type of theory

The use and role of theory varies in different research approaches, ranging from its complete rejection to being regarded as the most important component. Even among those that emphasize its importance there is considerable variability in what is meant by theory, and/or the most appropriate ways of using or constructing it. The most important definitions and uses of theory in the following discussion are:

- *Propositional theories*, which are loosely connected formal propositions about social phenomena (activities, events, structures or systems, beliefs). These propositions purport to 'explain' such phenomena, that is, offer a story about why or what caused them to exist, or how they came into being.
- *Theoretical perspectives or lenses* (such as Marxism, feminism, developmentalism, postmodernism) also contain even more broadly stated generalizations about

social phenomena. Their main problem is that they are often used to pre-interpret the social world in terms of this perspective or lens (Cresswell 2009) instead of relying on research evidence or data to uphold their claims. As such, they are relatively closed and resistant to evidence which challenges their assumptions and, in this respect, they are less useful for generating new ideas or advances in knowledge.

- *Substantive theories* are often formally stated but are directly linked with a substantive area, such as labour markets, professional conduct or ethnic relations. As opposed to propositional theories and theoretical perspectives, they are tightly focused and attempt to explain, or throw light on, a delimited aspect of social behaviour.
- *General theories* are integrated conceptual schemas that attempt to explain very general areas of social life and social behaviour (such as the relation between agency and structure or macro–micro aspects) or societal development. Examples are, Giddens' 'theory of structuration', Habermas's 'theory of communicative action' and Bourdieu's 'theory of practice'. Although such theories are often empirically applicable, usually they do not have a worked-through relationship with empirical research and are not designed to be used with it.
- *Deductive theories* are exemplified by Merton's middle-range theory (1968), which is derived from observations of empirical patterns (such as suicide rates). These lead to the deduction of logical propositions about what gives rise to (causes) such patterns – for example, suicide is related to how closely a person is integrated into their community. Deductive models are often used in conjunction with survey questionnaires and experiments and deal with the relations between discrete, quantitatively measurable variables like educational attainment, income or some attitudinal or behavioural regularity. Such quantitative measures can be tested for statistical significance while the theory specifies the (causal) relationship between dependent and independent variables, and can be tested in varying research circumstances.
- *Grounded theory* (GT) was originally formulated by Glaser and Strauss (1967) to counter what they took to be the weaknesses of deductive theories and general (or 'grand') theories. Grounded theory relies on an inductive procedure in which theory is grounded in data and directly emergent from data collection and analysis. In GT, theory does not 'determine' the research agenda in terms of testing or verifying a preconceived theory. Nor should theory or concepts be simply 'imposed' or 'forced' on empirical data.
- *Adaptive theory* has a close formative relationship with empirical research, as well as organic links with elements discussed below. Adaptive theory aims at producing explanations of social behaviour from, and during, empirical research, but does not rule out a role for deductive logic. It encourages the selective use of concepts from general theories as a means of improving the innovative potential of theorizing or 'explaining' social behaviour.

Despite the variety of theory types, some approaches are vehemently anti-theoretical and assert that social research should be humanistic and entail the collection of descriptive narratives of events, experiences and perceptions (Becker 1970; Rock 1979). On this view, social research is not about explaining social behaviour through a marriage of theory, concepts and empirical data. By contrast, investigative research is scientifically based on a mixture of theory, systematic methods of data collection, and explanatory objectives. In this sense, social research includes descriptive and humanist elements as integral parts of scientific explanation and method.

Model(s) of social reality (ontology)

If pressed, many researchers would claim that the 'reality' they are investigating has certain definite characteristics which, in some sense, influence research practice. However, there are many varied assumptions about the nature of social reality – what form it takes, its dimensions and properties, and how it impacts on research. Unfortunately, many if not most researchers are unaware of, or reject the importance of, these questions. Despite this, many approaches implicitly adopt a one- or two-dimensional ontology – model of social reality – which restricts the extent of their empirical coverage and their explanatory reach. IR is based on a multidimensional (domains) model of social reality which enables it to address causal questions and a wider range of empirical phenomena. IR recognizes that ontological models directly influence research practice and are decisively important for assessing the adequacy of research strategy.

Bedrock vision of social research

Bedrock visions of social research are encapsulated in answers to such questions as: What type of activity is social research? What underlying philosophy of social analysis does it reflect? What basic assumptions underlie particular approaches? Some approaches are based on a *natural* science view of the research enterprise, while others suggest that it is more appropriate to understand social life from a humanistic (interpretative) or even a 'pragmatic' perspective. Such beliefs and attitudes influence perceptions of research findings and methods of data collection and analysis. They raise questions such as: Should we be concerned about the objectivity, truth and validity of findings and knowledge in social research? Should research be about describing the viewpoints of different social actors in different contexts? IR employs a scientific mode of analysis that emphasizes methodological rigour and a systematic approach to data collection and analysis. However, it also relies on a central core of qualitative data to reflect the subjective understandings and experiences of research participants. IR attempts to build bridges between subjective, inter-subjective and objective elements of social life.

Objectives of research

What is the ultimate point of social research? This question is related to bedrock visions. Is the objective of social research to understand and interpret the meaning of the data that it collects? Or is it simply to collect and collate information about a topic of interest or a social problem? Is it about finding data that might support an explanation of social behaviour, or is it a purely descriptive exercise? Does social research attempt to inform social policy by evaluating a policy intervention? The objective of research may be to alter a work environment so that it functions more efficiently. This is true of 'action' or 'transformative research', in which the researcher is simultaneously a research subject. Alternatively, a research objective might be to eliminate or reduce discrimination towards oppressed groups or individuals, such as the disabled or the mentally ill. Such 'advocacy' and 'transformative' objectives are geared towards improving the lives and boosting the power of disadvantaged groups.

Despite the existence of many diverse objectives, it is important to sustain the distinction between political advocacy and the attempt to maintain objectivity of method. Political interests must not be allowed to compromise or override decisions about research methods or strategy. To elide the distinction in the manner that Creswell (2009) seems to suggest erodes the scientific neutrality and objectivity of data collection and analysis, and the principles of doubt and scepticism on which they should be based. Of course, many researchers are also political agents who want their research findings to contribute to humanitarian causes. However, the objective aspects of methods, strategies and analysis must never be undercut by political motivations. In this sense, the task of understanding the nature and causes of social phenomena is *logically prior to* and *independent of* attempts to empower research participants or to transform their circumstances.

Methods and strategies of data analysis

Approaches to research vary in their 'preferred' methods and strategies of data collection and data analysis. There are four broad possibilities. First, there are those that prefer purely quantitative data, methods and analysis coupled with 'a scientific approach'. Others opt for purely qualitative data, methods and analysis and emphasize a humanistic, interpretative vision of social research. A third possibility, 'mixed methods', arises from the mixing of quantitative and qualitative methods. With the mixed-methods approach, there are differences and disagreements about how to combine the methods, and whether it is possible to truly integrate them. A fourth position is a 'multi-strategy' approach (Layder 1993, 1998), which is the preferred mode for IR. This more inclusive position rejects the privilege of method (implicit in the mixed-methods approach) and elevates the importance of wider strategic elements (such as models of social reality and the 'internal' validity of methods and forms of knowledge). IR's multi-strategy approach injects a more nuanced appreciation of the social reality being researched, the problems being explored and the explanations being produced. The crucial point is that research should not be methods-driven. It should be problem-driven – where problems are not simply 'topics of interest' or 'social problems', but are concerned with explaining (the causes of) social behaviour and social processes.

Types of research design

Research approaches may be distinguished in terms of the 'research designs' they 'recommend', where designs are understood as the initial plans or blueprints of research. Designs vary in terms of initial departure points, whether the research commences with a tightly structured plan of action which is maintained throughout, or with a looser, minimal structure which changes and evolves during the research. Thus, research designs may be characterized as follows:

Pre-Specified ———————— Unfolding

Tight Structure ———————— Loose Structure

Inflexible ———————— Flexible

Where a particular piece of research sits along these continua will depend in part on its purpose. Thus, for example, research that sets out to test a (casual) relation between dependent and independent variables would need a pre-specified design (tightly structured) which is followed relatively inflexibly throughout. By contrast, research with a more open-ended agenda and purpose, such as gathering information on a topic or 'problem' about which little is already known, or where the objective is to generate theory, would be more unfolding and loosely structured. Investigative research designs interweave the exploration of a specific problem-focus with an attempt to explain social activity or behaviour. They also combine a strong emphasis on the generation of theory (or concepts) with some elements of theory-testing (verification). This amalgam includes elements of unfolding and pre-specification along with flexibility and stability within the same research designs.

Type and mode of data analysis

Research approaches differ in terms of how they deal with data analysis. One reason for this has to do with the type of data and method routinely used. For example, surveys using quantitative data (and statistical analysis) will require procedures of data analysis quite different from ethnographic research relying solely on qualitative data. However, other, more subtle factors are also important and are represented below.

Discrete ———————————— Continuous

Concept-centred ———————— Data-centred

Artificial Constructs —————— Real Life Events

Some approaches reserve data analysis for a discrete 'stage' or phase of the research process, most commonly at the end of data collection. In other approaches, it is begun as soon as the first data have been collected (sometimes even before the official start of the research – perhaps from a secondary analysis of existing data). With the latter, data analysis remains continuous throughout the research, not only at discrete or 'separate' phases. Although this is normally associated with more flexible research designs (and qualitative data analysis), in IR it is used in conjunction with more structured elements as well (in the form of a theory or 'conceptual scaffold').

Approaches also vary in terms of the way they regard data more generally. There are differing ideas about the 'fit' between data and the concepts they point to or indicate. This reflects a tension between regarding data as a reservoir of information or facts about the reality under study, or regarding it as resource for generating theory and concepts. Some approaches are more concerned with the conceptual than the empirical side of data analysis, and this often indicates an interest in theory. A greater focus on data as factual information frequently indicates a belief that theory is of little significance to research.

Finally, data analysis is influenced by the reality (the things, objects or phenomena, including human beings) that the data 'measure' or indicate. Some researchers treat reality as if it were composed of discrete 'variables', thus requiring a degree of control and artificiality (such as in experiments and surveys) in order to manipulate variables. At the other end of the scale, many approaches assume that social reality is comprised of 'relational processes' and so reject the relevance of the control and manipulation of variables. They deal with real, everyday situations which are emergent, unfolding and relational. Such processes cannot be analytically frozen or 'arrested'. IR, with its notion of entangled domains continuously unfolding along multiple dimensions, is in tune with the latter view, and differs markedly from approaches that are based on flat, one-dimensional models.

Verification and validation

Verification, validity and other quality assessments are necessary in all forms of research. In IR, validity – or the soundness and adequacy – of methods and data analysis is not exclusively defined in terms of quantitative criteria (as in variable analysis, surveys and experiments). With IR, processes of verification and validation are aspects of 'quality control', which are continuously tied to the unfolding dynamics of a particular research project and run throughout its entire length and duration. It may be true, as Tashakkori and Teddlie (2008) argue, that the term 'quality of inferences' is preferable to the (more restricted) definitions of validity provided by quantitative researchers. However, as a generic assessment of research quality, the notion of validity must not be abandoned. In this respect, the 'quality of inferences' does not take into account models of social reality, epistemic concerns or wider components of research strategy. While important, Tashakkori and Teddlie's 'mixed-methods' agenda concentrates solely on the problem of integrating quantitative and qualitative methods. Unfortunately, this restricts the debate about validity, verification and quality more generally to methods, whereas it should include the influence of models of reality (ontology) and problems concerning the integration of objective and subjective features of social life. In IR, quality control is an unbroken, adaptive process that begins from the initial statement of the research problem and continues through to the concluding report. That is, the explanatory spine or meta-argument of the research should organically bind all its 'phases' and not 'separate' them as discrete components.

The discussion now turns to a comparison of IR with other approaches and uses the above basic elements of research to assess their differences and similarities. It is important to bear in mind what was said at the beginning of the chapter. These depictions of other methods are not meant to be exhaustive overviews, 'introductions' or critiques for their own sake. They are selective appraisals intended to help position IR in relation to them so that researchers may either avoid the drawbacks or incorporate their strengths.

SURVEY RESEARCH AS MONO-METHOD

Survey research is often regarded (especially by its practitioners) as the 'gold standard' of social scientific 'method' because it appears to 'mimic' many features of the natural sciences. However, a major objection to this is that used as a mono-method, it makes no *attempt to 'capture' or understand the lived experiences of research subjects*, that is, *the existential core of social life*. In this sense, the relevance of survey research as mono-method is restricted to a disproportionately small area of social reality. On these grounds, the claim to represent the 'gold standard' of social scientific method lacks credibility because as a mono-method the survey arbitrarily rules out major features of social reality. In addition, it has little to say about social relations, social processes and causal mechanisms which embed the very variables that are central to it. But it is not possible to wrench discrete, measurable variables (like income or educational attainment, economic class, or opinions and attitudes) from their embedding contexts without overlooking the creative activities that underpin and reproduce them over time and space. Also, since variables are *defined in advance of research*, attention is diverted away from social relations, networks and causal mechanisms that might be of greater explanatory importance, but which only become apparent as they emerge from data analysis.

The combined force of these factors means that a reduction in analytical depth and explanatory power is a frequent trade-off from the wide and inclusive 'coverage' that can be achieved by large data samples. In addition, although 'fixed designs' allow survey researchers the time and resources needed to complete data collection and analysis (Robson 2007: 43), they also inhibit 'emergent' theory and concepts that are made possible via more flexible research designs. Inflexibility is exacerbated by the rigid use of probability (rather than non-probability or purposive) samples (see Chapter 3 for more detailed discussion), which restrict the possibility of additional sampling as a response to ongoing data analysis. The extent and likelihood of such problems are reduced by using surveys in conjunction with wider 'mixed strategies' and the more liberal and flexible use of non-probability samples – either instead of, or alongside, probability samples.

Of course, survey research does produce interesting and useful information of diverse kinds, for example, rates of social mobility, the distribution of social attitudes, opinions and practices, levels of income and education, racial or ethnic composition of populations, consumption of food or durables, the efficacy of drugs, rates of obesity, the incidence of mental and physical illnesses, or suicide rates. Surveys have also produced statistics on types of crime and criminal activity, and birth, marriage and death rates, even though it is well established that many such statistics suffer from problems of accuracy and reliability. However, as a mono-method, survey research has limitations of explanatory range, relevance and scope. Crucially, survey research by-passes and occludes the existential-experiential core of social existence and its connection with systemic aspects of society and processes. This necessitates a central role for qualitative data and greater personal involvement of researchers with research subjects.

Science and social research

With investigative research, a 'qualitative core' (of 'existential' or 'life-world' elements) serves as a central pivot around which multiple strategies (including survey methods) may be interwoven at appropriate junctures. In this sense, a qualitative core of data on psychobiography and situated activity is 'contained' within a surrounding envelope of data/evidence pertaining to social system aspects – social settings and contextual resources – which may require large swathes of quantitative data. With IR, the entangled domains model goes beyond the one-dimensional reality underpinning the survey method. Given the central importance of the experiential core, qualitative data and method must never be assigned an under-labourer role in relation to (allegedly) more 'scientific' survey and experimental methods (see Merton 1968; Goldthorpe 2000).

In marked contrast with IR, in surveys with large data sets 'rational actor/action' models are central (Goldthorpe 2000). As a methodological principle, it is assumed that human behaviour has a rational core, and that this is necessary to sustain the objectivity and rationality of science. But the exclusion of emotion and subjectivity mistakenly assumes that the epistemic objectivity of *scientific method* must also apply to its (ontological) *subject matter* – in order to be scientific. As Searle points out, 'the peculiarity of individual experiences does not place the subject of individual experience outside the realm of scientific inquiry' (1998: 49) and that 'the aim of science is to get a systematic account of how the world works. One part of the world consists of ontologically subjective phenomena, if we have a definition of science that forbids us from investigating that part of the world, it is the definition that has to be changed, and not the world' (1998: 114).

In the case of social science, it is misleading to assume a core of rationality in social action (activity, agency, social behaviour) because social action contains many subjective and emotional factors, alongside rational elements. To reiterate, the need for epistemic objectivity of method must not be confused with the necessity of an objective subject matter. Human social action includes a 'first-person ontology' (Searle 1998) and IR reaffirms this in the importance it accords to the experiential-existential core. However, in so doing it does not endorse the views of those researchers who argue that qualitative data should be judged in terms of aesthetic or artistic, rather than scientific, criteria. Such views make the obverse mistake of assuming that the subject matter of social life requires an epistemic subjectivity of method. They also lead to the idea that causal explanation is not relevant. But there is no reason why the scientific search for causality needs to be at the expense of descriptive or phenomenological accuracy. In essence, IR attempts such a synthesis. Of course, this is only possible in a context in which the aims and procedures of science are fully included in research methods and strategy.

THEORY-TESTING RESEARCH

Perhaps the most influential variant of theory-testing research is Robert Merton's 'middle-range' theory (1968), which shares many of the characteristics of survey research, such as the use of quantitatively measurable variables and the view that qualitative data lacks precision (and is thus destined to play a supplementary or 'under-labourer' role). The distinctive feature of Merton's approach is the deductive nature of theory construction. As an example, Merton takes Durkheim's (1952) study of suicide and its basis in the observation that in a number of different populations Catholics have a lower suicide rate than Protestants. This observation allows the researcher to make an empirical generalization, but in order to upgrade it to theory proper it must be derived from another set of propositions or assumptions. In the case of Durkheim these included the following:

> Suicide rates are related to the extent of social cohesion in a group.
>
> The more cohesive a group or community is the more psychological support it provides for group members.
>
> Catholic communities have greater cohesion than Protestant communities (closer ties and bonds).
>
> Thus, lower suicide rates should be anticipated among Catholics then Protestants.

Linking suicide rates with social cohesion allows connections with other areas, such as the family, marriage or occupation, and thus extends the potential scope of the theory. Merton also insists that a theory must be precise, determinate and predictive in order to increase its testability and reliability. Theory both guides observations and directs attention to relevant data, which serves to either confirm or falsify the initial theoretical propositions. If the theory is not confirmed, it may be possible to modify it so that it becomes more clearly concordant with the data. The point is to guide data collection via a preconceived, logically deduced framework of concepts, propositions and theoretical ideas. In this sense, theory is carefully worked out in advance of research, even though based on observations or empirical generalizations. The theory itself and its deductive logic take the lead in this, setting the criteria and standards by which it is to be judged. Deductive models raise the question of exactly how preconceived theories achieve a 'fit' with empirical data if they are formulated in advance of actual research.

This indeed is the opportune space that Glaser and Strauss (1967) took up with grounded theory (GT) and the idea that empirical data or evidence (especially in qualitative form) should have a freer hand in theory generation. IR also takes seriously the idea that data collection and analysis should be more actively and closely involved with theory- and concept-generation. However, it does not take the same route as GT (see Chapter 4) in that it does not reject the usefulness of preconceived theory as a means of stimulating the generation of theory from data. In this respect, IR recognizes the importance of co-opting aspects of general theory to enhance theory-generation. IR attempts to widen the net of possibilities for generating concepts and theory and so does not limit theory development to 'middle range' or 'grounded theory'. However, it does endorse the use of extant theory and concepts to 'dialogue' with ongoing data collection and analysis. In this sense, IR attempts to combine elements of theory-testing and theory-generation.

QUALITATIVE APPROACHES

Many qualitative researchers discount quantitative data and methods on the basis that 'scientific' precision is inappropriate to the subject matter of social research. They argue that human social behaviour is conscious, intentional and self-reflexive, unlike the inanimate objects of natural science which are moved by external forces, energies and processes. Shared meanings and interpretations distinguish social life from natural forces. As a result, research methods must tap into the experiences of research subjects (or participants) and reflect involvement and empathy with them in order to reflect their lived experiences. Thus, qualitative researchers typically favour semi-structured interviews, conversations, observation, participation and involvement with research subjects. Such methods are designed to capture the experiential substance of social life via the interpretative and empathic skills of the researcher. This is not possible by measuring mathematically precise variables that are said to externally cause social behaviour. Although all qualitative methods attempt to fulfil the above requirements, Cresswell (1998) has identified several different stands or styles of qualitative research: 'biographical studies', 'phenomenology', 'ethnography', 'case studies' and grounded theory.

Biographical studies

'Biographical studies' focus on individuals. This is unusual in social analysis, especially given that the social world is comprised of multiple relations between individuals and groups. As a 'method', it involves bringing together life documents, such as biographies, autobiographies and life histories, in order to provide interpretative accounts of the life experiences of individuals, emphasizing epiphanies, important turning points and achievements (Denzin 1989). The researcher gathers stories about particular individuals against the background of the wider socio-historical context. Given this focus, it is hard to identify distinctive differences in method between biographical studies and long-established 'biographical' strands in literary studies and journalism.

In one rather minor respect there is a link with IR, in so far as the domain of psychobiography focuses on the life course of individuals. An important difference is that 'psychobiography' is always relationally entangled with other domains (and their forms of power) and cannot be understood outside this multidimensional context. The point is that biographies do not supply their own conditions of existence, and thus are not self-explanatory. Individuals, their feelings and experiences, as well as their activities and interventions in social life, result from combined domain influences. It is not the case that individuals' psychological responses are simply determined by social forces, as many sociological approaches and research traditions seem to assume. However, in 'biographical studies', biographies are conceived as isolated and detached from other domains whereas, in reality, they should be understood as enveloped by, and intermeshing with, them.

Phenomenology, ethnography and participant observation

These strands of qualitative inquiry move away from a focus on single individuals to the lived experiences and interactions of many. In this sense, they represent the more 'traditional' subject matter of sociological analysis, and indeed, there is a considerable overlap between them when it comes to methods of data collection (interviews, observations and documents) and attitudes to theory.

Phenomenology as a form of qualitative inquiry requires the use of a specialist 'language' instead of commonplace descriptions. For instance, a phenomenological researcher might speak of 'essential invariant structures' or 'essences', such as a 'caring interaction in nursing', or of the 'lived experiences' of research subjects. Riemen (1986), for example, gathered patients' descriptions of their experiences of 'caring' or 'not caring' interactions while in hospital in order to understand 'the client's way-of-being-in-a-situation as it was actually lived and experienced by the client in interaction with the nurse'. Riemen concluded that 'the essential structure of a caring interaction ... was not defined by external criteria' (Riemen, 1986: 89). So apart from using technical language, the phenomenological viewpoint suggests that human social action is explainable exclusively in terms of the situated activities and lived experiences of the patients and nurses, rather than as an array of interconnected domains.

As qualitative methods, *ethnography* (Hammersely and Atkinson 1983) and *participant observation* (Rock 1979) also endeavour to depict the 'lived and perceived' worlds of research subjects by describing patterns, relations, habits, customs and values of social groups. Ethnographic or participant researchers make contacts and establish rapport with 'gatekeepers' and key members of such groups in order to tap into 'insider' knowledge of the group by having conversations, conducting interviews, and observing events and activities as well as examining cultural symbols and artefacts. Some ethnographies and forms of participant observation are simply designed to give a descriptive account of what it is like to be a member of a certain group, for example, the routines and conflicts experienced by jazz musicians (Becker 1963) or poolroom hustlers (Polsky 1967). Others focus on more specific problems, such as why and how workers become entrapped in, and 'negatively committed' to, low-status occupations with few intrinsic rewards, such as cocktail waitressing (Hearn and Stoll 1975).

Clearly qualitative studies of this kind are of central importance if social research is to address the 'experiential core' of social life. Since this is also a key part of the

IR approach to social research, it freely draws from ethnographic and participant observation methods and strategies. In contrast, by adopting an objective stance (surveys and experiments), it is difficult to achieve the intimacy and depth required to address the experiential dimension. Unfortunately, qualitative researchers often assume that the subject matter of social research is entirely inter-subjective and mistakenly believe that it must reject objective methods in favour of subjective ones. By contrast, IR includes attention to objective (systemic), subjective, and inter-subjective (or 'life-world') aspects of social life. So while qualitative approaches can supply vital data on the experiential core of social life, in a wider sense they differ markedly from investigative research.

IR employs multiple research strategies designed to cover those areas (psychobiographies, social settings and contextual resources) that are conspicuously 'missing' from qualitative approaches focused exclusively on inter-subjective aspects. Thus, IR might include quantitative data to depict wider social systemic phenomena (reproduced relations, organizations, forms of power and domination, discourses, values, class position) and employ them alongside qualitative data on the experiential core. In this sense, an interweaving patchwork of research strategies and interventions offers a more inclusive research net – in order to harness the complementary facets of entangled domains.

Second, IR underlines the importance of scientific criteria for assessing the validity of research methods and findings – criteria often rejected by qualitative approaches in favour of more subjective or aesthetic criteria. In this regard, there is not just one 'logic of inference', relevant to social science (that used in surveys; Goldthorpe 2000: 68), that qualitative approaches must adopt in order to qualify as scientific. Nor should qualitative approaches be considered only as 'an essential complement to survey research' (Goldthorpe 2000: 92), that is, as under-labourers to the allegedly more 'scientific' approaches (surveys and experiments). The idea of a one-dimensional logic of inference mistakenly assumes that social reality is homogeneous, rather than mixed and variegated. Scientific logics of inferences must be plural. They should embrace subjective, inter-subjective and systemic features of social reality, as well as recognizing their implications for methods and sampling (including reconciling 'population' versus 'problem' representativeness). Imposing a single logic of inference on to a variegated and multidimensional reality is not scientifically justifiable.

Finally, theory in qualitative research is often treated either as a sort of 'decorative addition' or as a bolt-on extra to the main descriptive narrative story. Alternatively, theory is dogmatically rejected on the grounds of being inappropriate to the humanistic character of social study (Rock 1979). IR emphasizes the importance of theory because the descriptive language of radical humanism suppresses sophisticated causal inquiry and stunts the overall accumulation of social scientific knowledge.

ACTION (OR TRANSFORMATIVE) RESEARCH

Action research demands a high level of commitment and involvement from researchers, although it is not wholly dependent on qualitative data and methods. It is frequently undertaken by professionals either to improve a work environment or to upgrade professional skills. Being a bona fide member of staff, the researcher maximizes her or his awareness of the aims and objectives of the research. In this sense, through researcher participation, research attempts to bring about social change from within. Action research is organized around continuous cycles of analysis, including goal setting, planning, evaluation and change. While not limited to qualitative evidence, it does play an important role in action research, with its focus on real-life, open-ended social situations involving the lived experiences of both professionals and their clients.

Houston (2010, 2015) has outlined some ways in which the investigative approach (especially the domains model) can aid action research into professional social work practice. For example, using social domains as a focus, an action research project can help identify relevant data, identify causal influences and suggest improvements to social work practice. As Houston notes, the principle of 'selective focusing' (Layder 1993, 1997) on particular domains may point to the importance of 'situated activity' for 'addressing how to improve relationships between residential workers and young people under their charge' (Houston 2010: 87). Houston also reminds us that it is important not to discount the influence of other domains, such as psychobiographies, social settings and contextual resources. In this respect, he points out that:

> attachment mechanisms within young people may be activated by the work of the staff; institutional rules may have a formative bearing on how the staff perform their role; and the politico-economic domain may generate constraints in relation to how work is managed and the availability of resources. (2010: 87)

Houston (2015) further illustrates how the social domains model can help shape social work practice in relation to the mentoring of students and novice social workers by more experienced colleagues, as well as supervision sessions in which feelings and facts about assessments are explored. He also notes that changing social work practice via social research (including emancipatory or anti-oppressive practices) requires an appreciation of the interplay between the personal and the political, and between human agency and social structure. The IR approach clearly enables the researcher to trace such empirical connections via the influence of social domains. In this sense, IR fits comfortably within the action research remit with its aim to facilitate professional change 'from within'. Having said this, it must also be borne in mind that IR is compatible with a broad range of research purposes and objectives.

USING IR: SOME PRACTICAL SUGGESTIONS

Using key dimensions of research, compared with surveys, quantitative data, theory-testing and qualitative approaches, it is clear that IR follows a quite distinctive path. On the other hand, IR should not be entirely cut off from the benefits offered by other approaches. In this sense, IR researchers are encouraged to borrow selectively and appropriately from other approaches in a manner that 'fits in' with their own interests and objectives. Further, where it is feasible they should engage in dialogue and/or cooperation between 'compatible' approaches instead of defending dogmatic or entrenched ideas. I believe that this is the best way to create genuinely cumulative scientific knowledge from social research. Having said this, of course, in this book I try to persuade readers and researchers of the advantages to be gained by using the 'investigative' approach. The following are some practical suggestions about how IR might be used to strengthen and enhance their own research. At the same time, it is designed to help them think of ways in which other approaches can complement, supplement or otherwise add value to their own research projects.

Dimensions of research

Being familiar with the core dimensions of social research prepares researchers to make practical decisions on some very important issues. For instance, with IR it is of crucial importance to decide what role theory will play in your research (and what 'type' you will use). In this respect, it is important to bear in mind that attempts to reject or circumvent these questions are non-starters. This is because such avoidant tactics immediately open up your research to charges of superficiality (no depth) and lack of analytical or explanatory substance, which weaken its adequacy and viability. Such criticisms will also reduce its acceptability by the wider academic community.

Similarly, having a clear (or at least clearer) idea of the model of social reality that lies behind and informs (explicitly or implicitly) your research can strengthen its claims about the completeness of data coverage and the rationales for the use of certain methods and strategies, including sampling techniques and data collection and analysis. Awareness of other dimensions, such as methods of data collection, research designs, forms of data analysis and quality control in different approaches, informs researchers of the need to inject consistency and clarity into project presentation, design and execution. You can be more confident of ensuring that the 'explanatory spine' of the project – the supporting arguments, claims and evidence that run through its whole trajectory – are logically coherent and robust.

Familiarity with 'objectives' and 'bedrock visions of research' enables you to demonstrate that you have convincing answers to questions such as: In what ways is your research based on sound scientific principles? What arguments and evidence would justify your answer? All in all, awareness of influential dimensions of research demonstrate the depth and penetration of your thinking about the project in terms of a range of analytical and empirical levels and aspects.

Surveys and quantitative data

Quantitative data and surveys can provide supportive and/or complementary evidence for IR research claims and findings. I have noted that when operating with IR there are dangers associated with using the survey as a mono-method. IR stresses the importance of using multiple strategies, methods and data sources to ensure (a) maximum high-density data coverage, and (b) comprehensive analytical saturation, resulting from a multidimensional domains model.

Ask yourself how can survey research add to my research? How will it strengthen, complement or supplement it? At the same time, you should bear in mind the following. First, IR requires some attention to the 'experiential core' of social reality via the use of qualitative data. Second, IR is adaptive and uses flexible conceptual scaffolds which 'evolve' during the unfolding of the research. As such, adaptive theory does not flourish if hampered by rigid commitments to propositional (or deductive theory) or inflexible research designs. Finally, it must be remembered that a central objective of IR is to add to knowledge by developing (conceptual/theoretical) explanations of data/evidence about social activity. This takes its emphasis quite away from the concerns of surveys and quantitative research, which concentrate on verifying or disconfirming relationships between variables.

Theory-testing

Given that theory and concepts are integral to IR, researchers must ask themselves: Are there aspects of theory-testing approaches that may benefit my own research project? To do this you must be clear how IR differs from theory-testing approaches. IR avoids, and sometimes rejects, many of the assumptions of theory-testing approaches. For instance, it rejects the idea that research should begin with a full analytical framework or set of propositions. Second, IR rejects the idea that the point of research is to investigate discrete and quantifiable 'variables' and to test-out the relationships between them. Third, IR does not assume that such relationships are the best or most appropriate causal explanations.

In sharp contrast, IR operates with provisional 'conceptual scaffolds' that evolve in relation to data collection over the entire course of the project. Second, IR assumes that the social world (social reality) is composed primarily of social relations, forms of power, domains, and so on, which cannot be understood as, or reduced to, discrete quantitative variables. This does not rule out the use of such variables in IR, but if they are used, they will not be the only or the main focus of study. IR assumes that a full causal explanation requires some role for qualitative method and data and an appreciation of the experiential core of social existence. Finally, this experiential core is a causal creation/product of domain influences, forms of power, social relations, discourses, and so on. Given these assumptions, you, as an IR researcher, must then decide if and in what sense 'modified' theory-testing principles may be of use. I have in mind here such things as the use of interim hypotheses about the relations between causal processes involving domain influences or the effects of power (on social activity/behaviour). In this respect, the logic(s) of scientific inference ensure that flexible changes in theory and concepts only occur alongside supportive evidence. Finally, quantitative survey data may be used to buttress the claims of the 'interim' or 'provisional' hypotheses just mentioned.

Qualitative approaches

Using IR automatically commits the researcher to at least some qualitative strategies, methods and data in order to study the experiential core of social life/reality. But IR is not in any sense simply a qualitative approach, for several reasons. First, it endorses and encourages the use of quantitative data, particularly as evidence of system phenomena (social settings, power and contextual resources). Second, the domains model encompasses but also goes beyond the inter-subjective realm on which qualitative approaches mainly focus. IR is concerned with combining the analysis of subjective, inter-subjective and objective (system) elements of the social world. Third, IR is committed to the scientific method of comparing theory against data or evidence, and a belief in objective methods of social research in relation to the qualitative and subjective aspects of its subject matter. Fourth, IR uses general theory as a source of orienting concepts to aid sampling, data collection and data analysis. It also uses extant or established theory and concepts to 'kick-start' theoretical innovation and conceptual generation. Finally, IR assumes that although description is an essential starting point, social science must go beyond it to produce adequate explanations of the behaviour/activities it investigates.

Despite these fundamental differences, there is still enough room for cooperation. In this respect, qualitative approaches can provide both rich data and sound data-collection techniques relevant to the existential core. However, of course, in so doing these must be at the service of explaining, rather than simply describing, ethnographic 'narratives', 'voices', or 'participants concerns' or 'doings'. Proper causal explanation must go beyond a focus on situated activity/behaviour in its own terms and include subjective (psychobiographical) as well as objective system elements (such as settings and contextual resources).

3

CASE STUDIES AND MIXED METHODS

CHAPTER CONTENTS

In this chapter I again draw on, and refer to, the research dimensions outlined at the beginning of Chapter 2. I first examine case study research, but I do not take a wide-angled perspective on it – this is not an attempt to summarize the topic as a whole. Rather, I focus on Yin's (2009) influential version of case study research, which, while possessing all its essential characteristics, also contains individual emphases and elements that are of especial interest for IR. The chapter then turns to 'mixed-methods' approaches and draws upon a wider array of authors. However, with both case studies and mixed methods, the discussions are specifically tailored to explore how IR is positioned in relation to them. There is no attempt to provide 'overviews' or 'how to' introductions to either approach. The main purpose of this chapter is to spotlight carefully selected aspects of both approaches to assess the extent of their compatibility with, and utility for, researchers using IR.

CASE STUDY RESEARCH

Yin (2009) defines the core elements of case study research in terms of: (a) a focus on specific cases; (b) existing in a naturally occurring contexts; (c) which are 'bounded'; (d) which are studied 'in-depth'; and (e) by using multiple sources. Case study research makes no attempt to control variables or to artificially construct research scenarios (like experiments). Rather, interconnections with real-life contexts are deemed to be 'highly pertinent' (Yin 2009: 18; Yin and Davis 2007). In these respects, case study research focuses in a more complex 'holistic' manner on real-life scenarios. Almost anything that exists in social life can be the topic of a case study, for example, decisions, individuals, organizations (such as a school or university), processes, 'programmes', a hospital ward or an office in a business (Yin 2009: 17). Cases are chosen because they represent some larger class of phenomena or are of interest because they are 'atypical' or 'extreme' in some way. Yin suggests, however, that it is a mistake 'to confuse case studies with ethnographies or with participant observation' or 'fieldwork'. 'A case study is an empirical inquiry that investigates a contemporary phenomenon in depth and within its real-life context, especially when the boundaries between the phenomenon and context are not clearly evident' (Yin 2009: 18). Nevertheless, it is necessary to distinguish 'data about the subject of the case study (the phenomenon) from data external to the case' and the need for 'spatial, temporal and other concrete boundaries' (Yin 2009: 32) in order to define the case.

Many of the above characteristics are shared not only by other 'versions' of case study research, but also with other – particularly qualitative – approaches. In addition, they complement many aspects of IR, and hence any 'mutual benefits' that are possible follow fairly straightforwardly. However, for present purposes, the most important aspects of Yin's version are its 'added extras', which make it very different from other versions. These include rigorous commitments to a scientific approach, to theory and theorizing, to specific logics of sampling, to replication and generalization, and finally to explanation and causality. In relation to these issues, there is much in common between IR and Yin's views (especially compared with other versions of case study research). On the other hand, there are also very sharp differences between IR and Yin's approach to these issues. The following discussion therefore concentrates on areas of overlap and disagreement.

Models of social reality and research practice

In the absence of any reference to an explicit model of social reality (of the kind discussed in Chapter 1), it is not clear from Yin's comments (above) how he envisages social reality in a more general sense, and which provides the overall context for the study of specific cases and in which they are embedded. This absence reaffirms the importance of taking such models into account and making explicit their implications for research practice. Thus, Yin leaves important questions 'hanging' and unanswered. For example: What social relations, mechanisms, forms of power and processes are involved? How do they operate? Are they emergent, differentiated or unitary? Do they articulate with structures, systems and reproduced relations? How are they related to creative and reproductive, cycles? To what extent do 'boundaries' delineate or define cases? In what ways are boundaries related to social processes and relationships? Are case 'boundaries' permeable?

In the absence of answers to such questions it can be legitimately argued that case studies have far more in common with other qualitative approaches than Yin admits. Mead (1967), Blumer (1969), Becker and Geer (1957), Garfinkel (1967) and Douglas (1977) all recognize the importance of 'naturalistic', or real-life situations, as opposed to observer-controlled variables and/or 'artificial', experimental constructs. They also evince a parallel concern with emergent social processes and relationships – as in Blumer's 'joint action', Glaser and Strauss's 'negotiated order', Garfinkel's 'local practices' and Collins' (2005) 'interaction ritual chains'.

On the other hand, for Yin, case study research is different in the sense that it is based on scientific, rather than humanistic principles, and stresses the importance of theory and the use of multiple sources of data. Combined with rigorous criteria of research quality and validity, case study research differs considerably from many qualitative approaches. Without an overall model of social reality, this somewhat odd and complex mix of influences simply increases the confusion about the links between case and context, and social relations and power.

Theory and theorizing in social research

Yin states that 'theory development prior to the collection of any case study data is an essential step' (2009: 36) and sharply distinguishes case studies from ethnography and grounded theory which 'deliberately avoid specifying any theoretical propositions at the outset of an inquiry' (Yin 2009: 35). In a similar fashion IR also relies on a fairly rigorous research design, but is based on a different view of theoretical preparedness. So although both approaches have a structured starting point, they have very different implications both for the unfolding of the research as well as for theory and explanation.

In summary:

> *Case studies* begin with a tightly formulated research design and a fully formed set of propositions (theoretical framework) to shape research design and guide data collection and analysis. Case study research is not concerned with the emergence of concepts and theory through adaptive responses to ongoing data collection. After data collection and analysis are complete, the original theory (framework) is confirmed, rejected or modified.
>
> *Investigative research* also begins with a tight-structured research design but operates in terms of a looser 'conceptual scaffold' – a cluster of concepts revisable in the light of ongoing data collection. Research explores a particular problem-focus (and core research questions). Data sampling, collection and analysis are in continuous dialogue with the conceptual scaffold. Eventually, there emerges a partly crystallized theory or explanation of the social behaviour under study.

In IR, there is greater leeway as to the form of the conceptual end-product, thus there is a greater range of variation in final explanatory outcomes. Why is this? The main reason is that while IR begins with a tight research design, its theoretical/conceptual starting point is more provisional. The initial scaffold defines a theoretical/analytical *problem-focus which is explored during the research.* A creative process, in which possible explanations of research data are examined in an open-ended manner, is set in train. The content and form of the scaffold evolves with the unfurling of the research itself, and its final form (and content) may be very different. The extent of its transformation depends on what is revealed in ongoing data collection and analysis.

Generalization, sampling and replication logic

Yin appears to recognize the need to break away from a view of social science based solely on survey and experimental approaches, and yet at the same time seems caught within their web. In surveys, 'statistical generalizations' are made about a population (or universe) on the basis of empirical data collected from a (representative) sample of that universe or population. In case studies, Yin states that it is a 'fatal flaw ... to conceive of statistical generalization as the method of generalizing the results' ... of research. The appropriate mode of generalization

> is "analytical generalization" in which previously developed theory is used as a template with which to compare the empirical results of the case study. If two or more cases are shown to support the same theory, replication may be claimed. The empirical results may be considered yet more potent if two or more cases support the same theory but do not support an equally plausible rival theory. (Yin 2009: 38)

In IR, analytical generalization is certainly more appropriate than statistical generalization. However, Yin's notion of analytical generalization derives from, and is limited to, experimental method (with its deductive logic, 'tight' causal relations between variables, and replication and comparison with rival theories). All of these have little relevance to IR, in which the emphasis is on conceptual innovation and theory generation. There is much less concern with the replication of results/findings and far more with seeking out new conceptual territory and interpreting evidence from innovative angles and fresh perspectives. Similarly, comparisons with 'rival theories' are less important because the researcher is not dealing with fully finished or closed/sealed theories. With IR, it is more appropriate to think of 'adjunct' or 'conjoint' explanations that may be of some use in building composite explanations. The IR researcher is looking for complementarities and potential alliances – that is to say, a 'constructive' response – rather than assessing or competing against 'rival' theories, which seems a rather negative (and often 'wasteful') response.

For its central data IR does not use statistically 'representative' samples, although they may play supportive or complementary roles. Rather, the point is to make generalizations about a deliberately targeted population. Samples are chosen because they contain data 'representative' of the problem-focus and core research questions (see the discussion of 'problem-sampling' in Layder 2013: 113 and 121), not because of the probability of their inclusion in some larger population. This is close to Yin's view where 'the investigator is trying to generalize a particular set of results to some broader theory' (Yin 2009: 43), rather than from a sample to a larger universe. However, Yin's notion of 'analytical generalization' is too narrowly tied to experimental methods which rely on artificially constructed scenarios, and the control and manipulation of variables. This is surprising since the explicit intention of case study research is to address 'real life contexts' (Yin 2009: 2). In this sense Yin's 'analytical generalizations' are difficult to apply to naturally occurring interactions – the stuff of everyday social life.

Explanation and causality

In Yin's view:

> internal validity is mainly a concern for explanatory case studies when an investigator is trying to explain how and why event x led to event y. If the investigator incorrectly concludes that there is a causal relationship between x and y without knowing that some third factor – z – may actually have caused y, the research design has failed to deal with some threat to internal validity. (Yin 2009: 42)

Here Yin equates explanation with 'event causality' (why event x leads to event y), which is dominant in experiments and surveys, but with IR, explanation is not tied to event causality. In event causality a discrete, antecedent event produces a subsequent event as a causal effect. However, as Searle (1998: 7) notes, many examples of cause–effect relations are not 'between discrete events ordered sequentially in time', as in the example 'the shooting caused the death of the victim'. What Searle calls 'non-event causation' is equally, if not more important, and he offers the following illustration:

> think of the causal explanation of the fact that the table exerts pressure on the rug. This is explained by the force of gravity, but gravity is not an event. Or think of the solidity of the table. It is explained causally by the behaviour of the molecules of which the table is composed. But the solidity of the table is not an extra event; it is just a feature of the table. (Searle 1998: 7)

If we consider examples from the social world, non-event causality is especially relevant to investigative research (Layder 1990: 92–104). For instance, social domains are contiguous and interdependent, so their (causal) effects on each other, and on social behaviour, are not separate events but a feature of their interdependence. In IR, for example, social behaviour is explained by the composite effects of social domains.

Description, explanation and analytical exploration

Yin clearly distinguishes explanatory from descriptive and exploratory studies as if they involved different analytical logics and practical procedures (Yin 2009: 42). In contrast, IR's central objective is to blend explanation, description and exploration as part of one overall investigative process. First, preliminary description is necessary because you cannot explain why something exists until you have a clear description of what you want to explain (the phenomena, the episode of behaviour), such as drug taking or mental illness and the typical settings in which it occurs. However, after a certain point, no amount of further description or observation will add up to an explanation, or a convincing set of reasons why the drug taking or mental illness occurred – what caused it. So descriptions are necessary but not sufficient, nor are they the same as explanations. In IR, there are no examples of purely descriptive research since, in itself, description is not enough. Thus, IR is heavily geared to offering a theoretical – or explanatory – account of empirical data/evidence.

Explanations here are not 'tight' and fully developed, they are more to do with the 'exploration' of an empirical problem-focus and core research questions. This requires a fluid and evolving conceptual scaffold, comprised of 'orienting concepts'. As such, 'explanations' are often loose-fitting, 'interim' responses to ongoing data collection and analysis. They are not permanent, unchanging edifices that 'dictate' how data and evidence is to be interpreted or understood. Rather, a conceptual scaffold is an orienting framework that is simultaneously 'ready' to accommodate unforeseen data. Comparing such 'scaffolds' (at whatever stage of their 'evolution') with so-called 'rival' theories is not particularly helpful. Rather, they should be viewed as part of the search for adjunct or complementary explanations.

Replication logic, prediction and reliability

Unlike Yin's version of case study research, IR does not rely on replication logic, prediction and reliability to develop a 'rich theoretical framework' from which to generalize the results of particular case studies and to allow 'scientists to cumulate knowledge' (2009: 44). For investigative research, the definition of social *science* must include the accumulation of knowledge across a wider body of social phenomena. Yin states that the 'replication logic' of experiments also underlies the use of multiple cases studies. 'Each case must be carefully selected so that it either (a) predicts similar results (a *literal replication*) or (b) predicts contrasting results but for anticipatable reasons (a theoretical replication). ... An important step in all of these replication procedures is the development of a rich, theoretical framework' ... which later becomes 'the vehicle for generalizing to new cases, again similar to the role played in cross-experimental designs. Furthermore, if some of the empirical cases do not work as predicted, modification must be made to the theory' (Yin 2009: 54).

Yin places a high value on replication and prediction as indices of good-quality research, 'positivist' science (natural science) and event causality. However, if social science is to include a qualitative assessment of the experiential core of social life, unfolding relations, variegated powers and non-event causality, then the limitations of replication, prediction and reliability become apparent. For example, the subject matter of investigative research is *situated social behaviour or activity* (such as how prisoners conduct their day-to-day business (with other prisoners, staff, and so on)) and would be the centre point of the research. In contrast, in case studies the problem-focus is likely to be a proposition, such as event x (the implementation of a programme, or policy, or the use of technology) either follows from, or leads to, event y. A typical example used by Yin is: 'one might consider the initial proposition that an increase in using a new technology in school districts will occur when the technology is used for both administrative and instructional applications, but not either alone' (2009: 54). Thus, further case studies might be selected to test out the predictions over various periods of time 'as support for the initial proposition'. As Yin says, 'if some of the empirical cases do not work as predicted, modification must be made to the theory'.

The issues of replication and prediction are far more important in this kind of event causality in the above example. But IR's focus on situated social behaviour has to be approached in terms of non-event or contiguous causality. This involves the analysis of relational processes which are continuously unfolding. In this sense, the study of situated behaviour does not lend itself to *exact* replication or prediction. With IR, it would not be fruitful to try to reproduce the exact research circumstances or to replicate or predict results/findings. With IR, the emphasis is more on the exploration of a problem-focus and searching out new concepts and theory, while at the same time gathering evidence that might or might not corroborate the results of previous studies. Decisions to modify extant theory/concepts are not made on the basis of 'predictions' or exact replications. Further research projects on the same or similar topics, areas or problems would be concerned with revealing (and more likely to yield) different findings and offer evidence requiring conceptual innovation.

In fact, the main emphasis in IR is away from the *exact replication* of previous research or research results, and towards achieving a close fit between concepts and data, and with developing coherent explanations. Of course, in order to check out validity, accuracy and reliability, IR researchers must clearly document research procedures, sampling techniques, and so on, so that later researchers can compare their own results and findings against them. In line with general scientific protocol, IR researchers must be subject to the scrutiny of the professional community. Careful documentation of research procedures (see Layder 2013) and providing transparent audit trails helps in the assessment of the validity of inferences, findings and conclusions by the wider research community.

MIXED METHODS

The use of 'mixed methods' or the combination 'of at least one qualitative and at least one quantitative component in a single research project or program' (Bergman 2008: 1) has been longstanding and widespread throughout the research community. However, an explicit approach labelled 'mixed methods' has only been developed relatively recently (see Tashakkori and Teddlie 2008; Creswell 2009) and the first specialist journal on 'mixed methods' was founded in 2007. The following discussion is not a systematic overview, but rather concentrates on particular aspects that serve to distinguish mixed methods from investigative research.

Multiple-strategies and mixed methods: some differences

Investigative research employs a 'multi-strategy' approach (Layder 1993: chapter 6). 'Multiple strategies', in common with 'mixed methods', assumes that it is possible, and often necessary, to combine the use of quantitative and qualitative methods and data in single research projects. However, 'mixed methods' overwhelmingly concentrates on technical problems of combining, integrating or blending quantitative with qualitative methods (Bryman 2008). 'Multi-strategy' research is concerned with more than methods and techniques. Thus, the role of social domains in explaining social behaviour is the most important driver and thrust of IR research, and is also the most important influence when it comes to combining quantitative and qualitative data and methods.

The domains framework provides practical vantage points at a more general level of analysis, allowing researchers to direct and organize the blending and integration of different kinds of data and method. In this sense, for IR, true integration cannot be achieved entirely in terms of mixing methods. A more general societal level of analysis is needed with a wider, more embracing, ontological viewpoint. Practically, domain analysis also allows researchers to filter empirical data findings and map their research implications. Thus, it is possible for IR researchers to make modest contributions to important issues, such as the 'agency–structure', 'macro–micro' and 'individual–society' problems. Such an opportunity is lost if methods integration is treated in isolation from these wider concerns.

Triangulation and density of coverage

In conventional usage, 'triangulation' is a validity check on research findings, which is achieved by using material from several sources (or viewpoints) to corroborate findings. Denzin (1989) distinguished between several types of triangulation – data, method, investigator or theory triangulation. IR adds a further type, 'social domains' triangulation, which importantly influences data selection and analysis, especially decisions about which kinds of data, and from which areas of social life or society, should be the point of focus, at which junctures in the research. These are in addition to the questions prompted by 'conventional' types of triangulation. Again, this form of triangulation may also condition the influence of the others since as well as including local project-specific issues, they also have more general analytical implications. Similar considerations apply to 'density of coverage'. In IR, this term not only applies to the dense compaction and volume of data (from study areas, physical 'sites' and sub-sites), but also to the more general properties and characteristics of the social domains from which they are drawn. In this sense, a social domain is not only a general, conceptual (and analytical) category of research, but also refers to an empirical, physically defined region of social life. Thus, in IR, 'density of coverage' refers both to general areas of social reality – domains – as well as specific (local) research foci.

Density of analytical viewpoints

In mixed-methods approaches, the density of analytical viewpoints is limited to matters internal to the project, perhaps in the guise of Yin's 'rival theories' (see previous section). By contrast, IR draws on conceptual elements and influences from 'external' resources, such as general theory and the domains framework. These are brought in not simply to dandify or to add superficial decoration to the findings, but actually to engage with local data and substantive concepts to create a synergy that contributes to the explanation of data, findings and conclusions. In this sense, researchers draw upon a wider variety of conceptual elements to understand how the conjunction of domains and local data and circumstances influences social behaviour. The dialogue, thus set up between internal and external resources, facilitates conceptual innovation and theory-generation. The wider variety of conceptual resources may also be used in dialogue with ongoing data analysis to test the viability of extant theory and concepts.

These concerns are conspicuously absent from mixed-methods approaches, focused as they are on practical and methods-driven issues. Inevitably this leads to a sort of 'methods reductionism', whereby explanation takes a back seat to the integration of quantitative and qualitative data and methods. Instead of narrowing research concerns, IR takes the opposite tack by considering an 'extra layer' of research calculations. It asks: What is the nature of the social reality being dealt with? How does it influence research questions, findings and conclusions? Such questions importantly filter and influence research decision-making about the appropriateness of methods, strategies and the meaning of data and concept–data linkages.

Research designs

Creswell et al. (2008) have set out templates for mixed-methods research designs. There are two main types: *sequential designs*, in which quantitative and qualitative data and methods are applied at separate points in time, and *concurrent designs*, which are conducted 'in parallel' or 'simultaneously', both of which could, in principle, be used in IR. However, IR's additional attention to social domains, and to both theory-testing and theory-generation within the same project distinguishes it with regard to design. As far as IR is concerned, the distinction between sequential and concurrent designs is potentially misleading. Of course, in one sense, all research can be seen as sequential because it unfolds in linear time. But for IR, there are two distinct levels of analysis – internal and specific, and external and general – operating simultaneously in particular projects. Such a two-tier model cannot be reduced to an 'either/or' status of sequential or concurrent – they operate in both modes simultaneously.

Also, mixed-methods writers suggest separate designs for 'explanatory' and 'exploratory' research (Creswell, et al. 2008: 118), but offer little advice either on the use of theory or on theory construction. Also, since sequential designs require the sequencing to be pre-specified before the start of research, they consequently lack the flexibility necessary to make adaptive changes once underway. By contrast, IR research designs are explicitly geared to blending exploratory, explanatory and descriptive objectives.

Although emergent and unfolding designs play important roles in IR, they are combined with a pre-specified but provisional conceptual scaffold. This provides initial order, direction and momentum for the project, but then adapts and evolves into different forms with ongoing data sampling and analysis. With designs of this kind it is vital that the application of 'validity' and 'quality' criteria are of the 'continuous' rather than the discrete kind. They must embrace all phases and aspects of the research, not simply the integration of data and methods. These include prior assumptions, presuppositions and propositions (about the nature of social reality and how we come to know it) as well as the ways in which they influence subsequent phases and assumptions. That is, inferences and conclusions must be evaluated in the light of such prior assumptions and not simply in terms of mixing methods, or even the application of mono-methods. In the case of IR, for example, there is a need to distinguish between a more general subject matter (the influence of domains) and a specific subject matter (evidence and data). By prioritizing the integration of methods and data, mixed-methods approaches ignore the 'silent' or 'implicit' validity claims and assumptions built into research designs.

Pragmatism as a philosophical rationale for mixed methods

Mixed-methods practitioners cling to a form of pragmatist philosophy (Rorty 1979) as a justifying rationale for research designs, decisions, practices and procedures. This is a highly problematic 'version' of pragmatism, which at one time was used strictly to characterize the work of the American philosophers Peirce, James and Dewey, but now the term is linked with a diversity of views and topics (including ethics, politics and environmental ethics), arguments and methodologies which often have little in common with each other (Talisse and Aikin 2008). Such a state of affairs lends weight to the charge that pragmatism is inherently vague and ambiguous, especially as it relates to mixed methods (Bergman 2008). All too often this state of affairs has the effect of concealing its weaknesses and contradictions.

For IR, both the prior assumptions and subsequent findings of social research are 'forever incomplete', because 'the approach requires that knowledge be viewed as always potentially revisable in the light of evidence which may be brought to bear and as a result of innovations in conceptualization and explanation' (Layder 1998: 176). Theory and theorizing are also 'inherently unfinished, incomplete' and 'interim products' because they too can be 'revised and reformulated in the light of empirical evidence and further insights and arguments' (Layder 1998: 178). While IR is based on systematic principles, it gives rise to research findings and knowledge that are provisional and open to challenge, improvement and disproof or refutation by dint of empirical evidence. By any stretch of the imagination, such knowledge is, and cannot be, absolute, permanent or universal. Furthermore, the fact that IR is not based on pragmatism refutes the claim that pragmatism uniquely ensures that mixed methods deliver open and improvable knowledge.

In line with arch pragmatist and postmodernist ideas about 'post-truth', mixed-methods researchers insist on rejecting the search for what Rorty (1979) calls 'objective truth'. This is a disastrous move which in itself is based on the misconception that truth is necessarily a search for 'absolute' rather than 'limited and provisional' knowledge, of the kind alluded to in the previous paragraph. Even worse, mixed-methods pragmatists insist that 'truth' be replaced by other words and phrases such as 'practical adequacy' or 'what works in practice', or by effective solutions to practical research problems. Unfortunately, these 'alternatives' do not hold water because they exclude crucial epistemic aspects such as the validity of research design, models of reality, research 'problems' and prior assumptions about the most appropriate methods and strategies of data collection and analysis. They also exclude practical concerns about the validity of research practices and findings, such as: Do they make sense in terms of their applicability in specific empirical circumstances? Are they likely to achieve goals which cannot be measured entirely in practical terms, such as to enhance social integration or to reduce inequality? Are they morally and ethically justifiable? After all, the Holocaust was 'a practically adequate solution' to the problem of exterminating human beings!

The confusion of truth with 'absolute truth' chimes with the pragmatist claim that truth can never be conclusive since all knowledge constantly shifts according to fashions and social currents. But if this were the case, we could never know which of the many was the 'better truth' in any given social context and thus we would have no means of deciding which to choose. Since all practical solutions to a research problem would be considered equally valid – as having the same truth value as each other – basing decisions and actions on them would be impossible. If we cannot ask 'which is the better truth?' or 'are we not at least engaged in the search for a qualified version of it?', we are trapped at the level of practice. We can only indicate a range of practical solutions to practical problems. We cannot judge the appropriateness of the solution, or the way the problem is conceptualized. Nor can we posit that there might be problems that cannot be defined simply in terms of practical criteria. That is, we cannot speak of non-practical problems because this would require reference to higher, non-practical principles, such as moral, ethical or intellectual objectives or purposes (the Holocaust, again, offers a pertinent example).

By recklessly abandoning truth, theory and abstract principles and instead embracing 'practical adequacy', mixed-methods pragmatists are unable to tackle or resolve crucially important problems and issues in social research today. For instance, by rejecting all forms of dualism as red herrings or blind alleys, mixed-method pragmatists simply circumvent the problems that dualism raises and prevent any genuine solutions being sought. Such avoidance blocks the insight that the agency–structure or the macro–micro dualisms are better understood in terms of variegated, multidimensional models of social reality (ontology) – as in the domain framework. Ironically, pragmatism fails to grasp the practical insight that the most pressing problems of social research stem from the fact that dualism shuts down areas of social reality that should be opened up to empirical research. Finally, pragmatist ambivalence towards theory is problematic for its scientific credentials. All sciences rest on an explanatory foundation, and the distinction between theory and empirical evidence. Pragmatist's indifference to theory, epistemology and ontology undercuts any claims to social *science*.

USING IR: SOME PRACTICAL SUGGESTIONS

Using the key dimensions (outlined at the start of Chapter 2) as points of comparison, it is apparent that while IR is an independent approach, it also draws on many of the strengths of other approaches. As with previous chapters, the assumption here is that researchers will *borrow selectively* and appropriately from other approaches. For instance, a researcher might use some aspects of mixed methods, while rejecting pragmatism as a rationale, and instead adopt IR principles in conjunction with (other aspects of) mixed methods. Thus, my intention has not been simply to highlight IR's advantageous features in order to force an either/or decision – either adopt IR or another approach. The following suggestions and advice are therefore intended for those researchers who remain open to the influence of other approaches. Cooperation, openness and dialogue are the watchwords of genuinely scientific and cumulative research knowledge. Although I dealt with several issues about the use of theory at the end of Chapter 2, the discussion in this chapter has raised a number of additional problems. These primarily concern your general attitude to theory and its place in your current project.

Attitude to theory

Ask yourself: What is my attitude towards theory with regard to the research I have in mind? Do I want my research to contribute to theoretical as well as empirical knowledge (evidence, facts, data, information, and so on)? In what ways can I contribute to theoretical knowledge through empirical research? There are three options:

a) Do you want to use theory to guide and inform the empirical data you gather? This includes using it as a framework for interpreting patterns in the data and for helping to shape findings and conclusions.
b) Do you want to be more involved, both practically and imaginatively, in generating theory and innovative concepts?
c) Would you prefer-some balance between (a) and (b)?

I shall assume that you want your research to contribute to the stock of theoretical as well as empirical knowledge, but you are undecided how to go about it. If you decide that you don't want your research to contribute to theory, then IR is not for you. However, before moving on, you should reflect on the consequences of this decision for how your research will be perceived. Because of its importance, it is worth reiterating that it would be very easy for those who judge the research to perceive it as lacking explanatory depth. Your research will also be vulnerable to the criticism that it lacks a scientific basis since science relies on theories as vehicles to explain empirical evidence or data. In this sense, theory provides answers to questions about why the data forms certain patterns, and how they are caused. In short, your research may be perceived as descriptive, but not explanatory, and thus as offering a relatively superficial account.

IR can help with all three options (a, b, and c) because it is generally theory-friendly and would be of some use regardless of your specific requirements. However, IR is probably of most help for those choosing option (c), who wish to combine elements of (a) and (b) within the same project. In this respect IR provides opportunities for blending extant theories and concepts with a search for innovative concepts and fresh modes of explanation.

Research problems and questions

Many of Yin's views on case study research are admirable, particularly the grounding in science and the emphasis on the importance of theory. Nevertheless, there are also crucial differences with those that underpin IR. First, Yin's view of science is based on quantitative, survey and experimental approaches. IR's notion of science is based on a more nuanced and embracing view of social reality. Social 'science' must acknowledge the decisive importance of qualitative data, methods and strategies in order to investigate its experiential core, while social processes, domain influences and social relations of power cannot be 'measured' in the same sense as discrete, quantifiable variables. Such a notion of science must underscore the objectivity of its method while recognizing that its subject matter contains 'combinations' of subjective, inter-subjective and objective (system) elements.

The same caveats apply to the use of theory in social research. Yin seems rigidly committed to propositional theory (Chapter 2). However, IR enables researchers to stray beyond its confines while respecting its underpinning rigour, reasoning and logic. From the point of view of IR, there are several problems with propositional theory. First, it is linked exclusively to event causality (event x follows from, or leads to, event y) and this makes it impossible for researchers to produce dense, qualitative accounts of situated behaviour/activity. This falls short of the claim that case studies are about real-life contexts, since their study would require non-event causality to capture the irreducible quality of the unfolding processes involved in socially situated behaviour.

Second, because of its need for relatively fixed designs, propositional theory makes it very difficult for researchers to generate theory or concepts, which requires flexible designs as well as continuous data sampling, collection and analysis. Further, the use extant theory or concepts in response to ongoing data collection is severely hampered by the constant need to refer data and findings back to the central proposition, in order to judge whether they verify or disconfirm it. Finally, propositional theory does not allow any input from ontology – models of reality – whereas IR enables researchers to tap into underlying aspects of reality which, if acknowledged, can and should influence the formulation of research problem and questions. The same is true for researching causality. Propositional theory assumes that causality is best expressed in terms of precise relations between events or variables, whereas IR traces non-event causal relations at both general analytical and local empirical levels.

Case studies and investigative research

The serious differences identified above (along with an over-reliance on prediction and replication) would seem to stand in the way of cooperation and dialogue with IR. However, my arguments are not aimed at case study *per se*, but rather at some aspects of Yin's version of it. Three possibilities seem to present themselves.

First, there are several versions of case study research other than Yin's that depend on more general characteristics, such as a focus on bounded, specific instances, real-life contexts, in-depth study, and the use of multiple sources or methods. They are often much looser versions than Yin's with regard to propositional theory, science, prediction, replication, and so on. Thus, many case studies can complement or supplement research based on IR. In this respect, case studies can be influenced by IR principles and in this sense regarded as an alternative to Yin's version. Finally, there is the possibility of a hybrid, containing elements from Yin alongside elements of IR. Of course, this will have to avoid obvious clashes of ideas, principles and practice, but is possible, for example, if propositional theory is used separately but in parallel with adaptive theory – as complementary or supplementary to each other.

Mixed methods and IR

Of course, ensuring that methods are properly integrated is an important task in social research, and mixed-methods approaches have made great strides in this direction. There are several fairly straightforward ways in which IR can work in tandem with or alongside mixed methods in an effort to contribute further to methods and data integration. However, from the point of view of IR, there are some dangers to be avoided. First mixed-methods pragmatism, with its rejection of any notion of the search for limited empirical truth, seems to undercut the idea of scientifically robust forms of verification and validation. Second, IR regrets the tendency for mixed methods to become myopically concentrated on technical issues of method to the exclusion of wider problems, including the role of theory, the nature of social ontology – models of reality – and the nature of social 'science'. From an IR viewpoint, such issues should be acknowledged and engaged with in order to unleash the potential for developments in research strategy and for cumulative knowledge.

Does your research have solid foundations?

Ask yourself: How can I base my research on solid foundations? Is it firmly grounded in a coherent model of social reality? Is it based on a solid bedrock vision of social research that leads to valid, reliable and accurate results? Does it embrace all facets of social reality? Is it based on sound epistemological principles? Are all these features open and inclusive rather than closed and dogmatic? Do they support the idea that knowledge is provisional and revisable in the light of empirical data/evidence?

Sound research cannot be achieved by simply plucking a research question or problem 'out of the air', applying 'practically adequate' methods of data collection, and then drawing conclusions about the data, information or evidence you have collected. It cannot be simply based on expedient solutions to practical problems – as in pragmatism. But neither should research be limited by the application of a set of inflexible, 'absolute' principles. Nonetheless there must be *some principles* and prior assumptions that govern the implementation of research methods and strategies and which serve as their justifying rationale. So there must be a balance. The principles and assumptions that form the foundation of the research should not be so intransigent as to be unable to accommodate *in situ* unforeseen circumstances, data and changing ideas.

In this respect IR offers a balance between these two extremes. I am not claiming that it is the only possible approach that can offer this, but it does offer a genuinely balanced approach. This is because within its terms of reference (for example, the analysis of social domains, its scientific basis, and use of multiple strategies) it reconciles a number of seemingly competing approaches by using them in a complementary manner. Openness and inclusiveness are built into its assumptions about social reality, and the best ways of analysing and researching it. It accesses general issues and problems, such as the nature of social reality, and embraces a multidimensional view (entangled domains) in opposition to 'reducing' social reality to a single dimension or conceptual principle. Thus, the domains model ensures a dense and adequate data coverage of the social reality under research scrutiny, whereas one-dimensional approaches routinely omit important areas (slices of reality). Second, such a model offers a viable explanatory account of these areas of social reality and of social behaviour. Third, it guarantees that enough space is allowed for conceptual innovation, new angles and directions of analysis. Only by building on solid foundations will your research be robust enough to produce a dense empirical coverage and a proper explanatory account of the research problem.

In the light of the above comments, ask yourself: How can I ensure that the more practical aspects of my research – the design, methods of data collection and forms of data analysis – are deeply rooted in solid but flexible foundations (such as those above)? Are they rooted in appropriate models of social reality, and not simply governed by practical or technical criteria?

4

THE LIMITATIONS OF GROUNDED THEORY

CHAPTER CONTENTS

While it can be argued that all research is, or must be 'investigative' in nature, more considered reflection reveals that this is not necessarily the case. Of course, 'investigation' as a noun is often used loosely to refer to the activities involved in the general garnering of evidence ('clues' in criminal investigation) for an empirical research project. However, in a more technical sense the essence and 'propulsion' of investigative research is provided by its ever-present openness to the possibility of new forms of explanation, new ideas, fresh evidence, or new angles on evidence. With many other approaches, an open-search element quickly falls to the wayside. Sometimes, 'openness' is eliminated even before data collection gets underway, and exists only in a preliminary phase of project design (as with many quantitative approaches). In other instances, openness is jettisoned after some initial data collection and analysis have firmed-up the main conceptual, theoretical or explanatory focus (as is typical of many qualitative approaches).

'Grounded theory' approaches attempt to continuously attend to theory-generation or discovery, and in this chapter I compare them with investigative research. In the first part of the chapter I focus on Glaser and Strauss's original version of grounded theory (with particular reference to Glaser's interpretation) with a view to identifying its weaknesses, from an IR perspective. The second part of the chapter examines Charmaz's so-called '21st century constructionist GT' which, she claims, is a more 'advanced' version than Glaser's. I argue that although Charmaz offers minor advances, in fact (and as is true with all versions of GT) it shares exactly the same fundamental limitations as Glaser's because they are intrinsic to GT's basic assumptions. Charmaz's claims to have produced a more advanced GT only serve to highlight some of the added advantages of the IR approach in terms of the depth and power of its empirical coverage and explanatory reach. The chapter thus ends with a discussion of some of the practical research differences IR makes in relation to data sampling, collection and analysis, as well as to theory-and concept-generation.

GROUNDED THEORY: GLASER AND STRAUSS

The 'grounded theory' (GT) approach (Glaser and Strauss 1969) differs from investigative research (IR) in that GT is *solely* concerned with the generation of new theory from data. In this sense, GT excludes all extant (received or 'preconceived') theory and concepts – in short, anything that has not been produced under the strict auspices of GT method. With IR, this is regarded as a waste of good theoretical ideas, especially those that have been developed from previous (non-GT) research.

Investigative research attempts to harness the explanatory potential of other research strategies and forms of theory development. This raises more general questions about the role of concepts and theory in research firmly anchored to data collection. For example: In what sense can theory and concepts be 'discovered' as a by-product of data analysis? Should researchers rely on extant concepts and theory to help code and analyse data? Is it possible to generate theory directly from data, as many exponents of GT claim? Do concepts vary in terms of the kind of social reality to which they refer?

INVESTIGATIVE RESEARCH

Investigative research is governed by two principal objectives, which are achieved by specifically tailored, but flexible, designs. The first is to retain at all times an open attitude towards the construction or discovery of new ideas, concepts and theories (which form the basis of explanations or answers to questions and problems). The second is to maintain this attitude in relation to *ongoing* data collection and analysis. Both objectives should be pursued simultaneously without privilege or priority being accorded either to theoretical/conceptual matters or to issues of data collection and analysis. It is of the utmost importance that both are attended to concurrently, so that they are kept in a tight allegiance at every point in the unfolding of a research project. However, the emphasis on the emergence of new concepts and theory does not mean that investigative research is *only* concerned with innovative ideas or discovering new explanations. In fact, accumulated knowledge and theories from previous studies also play a central role.

The essential rule of thumb here is not to preclude (and thus exclude) potentially useful new ideas or 'angles' on data analysis *at any point* in a project – either at the beginning or throughout its execution. In this respect, the antennae responsible for detecting, and developing, potentially new and interesting concepts (and theory) are built into initial research designs. Moreover, while these initial designs are highly dependent on accumulated knowledge (extant or received concepts and theories), ongoing adaptive flexibility ensures that they are not permanently 'frozen' into the research project and its unfolding trajectory. There is no absolute fixity of the initial research design or strategy, nor is there any forcing or imposing of theory and concepts during data analysis. The flexibility of design removes blockages to the emergence of theory and concepts that are likely to result from a rigidly imposed, preconceived design or explanatory framework. All concepts – extant or emergent – should be allowed to adapt as a flexible response to the analysis of emergent data.

ESSENTIAL DIFFERENCES BETWEEN INVESTIGATIVE RESEARCH AND GROUNDED THEORY

There is a surface similarity between IR and the GT approach, in terms of a focus on generating novel theory in conjunction with research data. However, beyond this there are vast differences between the approaches. Unfortunately, some have mistakenly imagined that IR is simply a derivative or variant of grounded theory. For instance, Glaser himself (one of the originators, along with Strauss, of GT) perceives my 1998 book *Sociological Practice*, as a misguided attempt simply to 'adopt and adapt' the basic elements of grounded theory by dubbing GT 'as adaptive theory with no explanation or definition' (Glaser 2001: 77). Glaser simply ignores the fact that I was offering a radical alternative to GT and moving away from what I regard as its in-built limitations. As a corrective to such misunderstandings, I want to clarify the essential differences between investigative research and grounded theory. This involves drawing attention to the vast epistemological and ontological chasm between IR and GT, along with more prosaic and practical differences – in research design, sampling, coding, and modes of data collection and analysis. This will serve to highlight the distinctive and unique aspects of the investigative approach.

Key differences point by point

Models of social reality

The bedrock differences between IR and GT lie in their fundamentally different views and models of social reality (social ontology). IR operates with an expanded and more inclusive model of social reality. For GT, social reality is limited to the inter-subjective realm – of 'participants concerns' as Glaser (2001) phrases it – and thus, social research is focused on social interaction and person-to-person relationships in particular empirical areas. This emphasis is a reflection of its very close links with 'symbolic interactionism' (based on Mead's (1967) and Blumer's (1969) work, among others). While social interaction and person-to-person relationships (largely covered by what I previously refer to as the 'experiential core') are crucial to many forms of social research, IR also recognizes the influence of other social domains for an overall explanation. These include individual psychobiographies, situated activity, settings and contextual resources, all of which are relatively independent of each other, while also deeply intertwined and mutually influential. Importantly, such elements of social reality *are not levels of analysis, but rather interconnected domains of reality* whose combined effects are overlooked by GT with its exclusive focus on one domain – situated activity. In this sense, GT operates with a one-dimensional ontology while IR assumes a multidimensional and variegated ontology.

Types of concept: veracity and validity

A consequence of these profound differences in underlying models of social reality is that there are also wide disparities in epistemology, that is, the knowledge assumptions relevant to, and underpinning, the models. How are concepts (and theories) formed, especially in relation to data-gathering research? What ensures the veracity, validity and adequacy of such concepts? Again, IR is more broad-ranging and inclusive, allowing for several distinct types of concept pertinent to different domains. Thus, in IR, there are 'action' or 'behavioural' concepts (those referring to individuals and their psychobiographies as well as to situated activities) as compared with 'system' concepts (those pertinent to settings and contextual resources). Perhaps, most importantly, there are 'bridging' concepts, which link action and system concepts. Thus again, the research, theory and concepts of GT are restricted to one domain – that of situated activity (or the inter-subjective realm).

Research problems

This brings us to an associated issue. IR addresses a wider range of research problems than GT, which is limited to identifying the 'main concerns' of the participants and how they resolve them (Glaser 2001). In contrast, for IR, a comprehensive explanation (or even description) of social behaviour must take account of all contributory influences – including that of other domains – and not simply be limited to 'the main concerns of the participants, and how they resolve them'. Thus, a full explanation must take into account unique psychobiographies where they are relevant, including the variable capacities, attributes and powers of individual participants. Psychobiographies cannot be written-off as of no consequence to social outcomes, or dissolved and absorbed into local interactions or social practices. Second, 'situated activities' must be understood in a more rounded sense than simply the participants' main concerns – they must include psychobiographical inputs. Third, there must be an assessment of the relatively independent contributory influence of at least one 'core' or several cross-cutting social settings in which the activity or event occurs (particularly as it affects situated activity and individual psychobiography). Fourth, there must be an examination of the influence of relevant contextual resources (discourses, media, cultural meanings and symbols, gender, class, status, age, disability) *to determine the extent to which they are pertinent* to explaining the data and/or observed behaviour. There is no suggestion that any of these factors (domains) should be assumed a priori to be causally (or analytically) relevant in advance of data collection, but neither should this possibility be completely ruled out. Finally, the forms of power and temporality that run through each domain should be considered as possible explanatory factors, especially where they combine in a complex fashion in particular empirical circumstances.

In short, the problem foci of IR research are many and varied, reflecting the variegated nature of the social landscape in the form of empirical data as well as in terms of theory and concepts. In IR this leads to a search for multiple causal influences (but not a priori causal relations) on social behaviour and other social phenomena. The problem-focus of GT is singular and exclusive, not only to the interpersonal domain but, in Glaser's case, to one slice of this domain – the 'participant's main concerns and how they resolve them'. This reflects GT's one-dimensional social landscape and myopic preoccupation with (one aspect of) social interaction.

Research and the analysis of power

Investigative research centralizes the importance of power for all empirical research. For GT, power is scarcely, if at all, mentioned as relevant (particularly in Glaser's 'pure', 'original' version). In GT terms, concepts of power must be considered as 'preconceived' or 'received' (as opposed to 'emergent') and can only be 'imposed' or forced on data, and thus they must be rejected as 'un-grounded'. Only concepts that 'earn their way into' the analysis can be deployed or said to be truly emergent. For pure GT, power is both a generic and an a priori concept and thus is disqualified as 'emergent' or grounded. By contrast, IR squares up to the empirical reality that power exists everywhere in society, as endless empirical instances demonstrate, from the seemingly insignificant interactions of everyday life to the highest levels of political and economic power. Unlike Foucault (1980), however, IR assumes that power is not everywhere the same. Power is not a unified phenomenon, it is not generic in form. Power – its forms and influences – varies from domain to domain and combines in a multiplicity of ways to produce social outcomes. This means that the operations and consequences of power must be taken into account from the outset of a research project.

There are later, 'amended' versions of GT (for example, Charmaz 2006) that claim that a 'modified' GT enables it to incorporate power as a form of interactive negotiation (as in symbolic interactionism; see Luckenbill 1979) which can be played out individually or collectively. However, structural or systemic forms of power cannot be reduced to interactional and 'negotiated' terms. Importantly, they depend on prior conditions of access to forms of authority and control (in social settings), and to material and symbolic goods and resources (as reflected in asymmetries of a class, gender, age or ethnicity; see Layder 1985 and 2004). Charmaz does not recognize variations in the reality and consequences of power according to the social domain from which it derives, and especially when different domain powers combine in influence. In IR, the powers of (unique) individuals are very different from, but no less consequential than, power as it manifests in situated encounters (Layder 2004) in which several individuals share and simultaneously compete for power resources. But personal power (based on capacities, feelings and motivations) and interactive power (the social outcomes of situated activities) cannot be reduced to each other. They are different but interconnected 'types' of reality with their own properties and effects and signified by the term 'social domains'.

Similarly, the collective and agential power of commercial organizations, such as McDonald's (Ritzer 2011), or governmental bureaucracies (taxation offices or public hospitals) and the 'formal' powers of those working within them, are quite different again. Such power cannot be treated (analytically or empirically) as identical to power in situated encounters, or to the unique personal powers of individuals. Many social settings manifest organizational forms of power, while other settings exhibit less formal and more 'disorganized' or 'contingent' forms of power. The powers embedded or inscribed in social settings cannot be reduced to any of the other domain forms – individual, interactive or contextual. 'Contextual' powers are society-wide asymmetric distributions of resources such as material and symbolic capital. Unequal access to them influences individual behaviour and psyches. Although 'groups' or other 'collective agents' have power, again it is based on the wider asymmetric distributions of resources.

In sum, power is not generic, nor do any of its domain forms operate alone. Different forms of power intermingle with each other continuously and variably, while a more precise analysis will depend on evidence, data or research findings. Describing and explaining the influence of interlinked domain powers are central to investigative research. Data collection and analysis are shaped around the empirical evidence of power in every 'nook and cranny' of society (see Nye (2011) for an analysis of power at the level of nation states in the global age). In stark contrast, GT in its original form suggests that core concepts and their properties can only be 'earned into' a theory on the basis of emerging data. In IR, power does not have to be 'earned into' research analysis because it is already embedded in every facet of social life. Empirically, however, the point of investigative research is to reveal how the effects of different domain powers work themselves out in varied social circumstances and with respect to specific research problems. There can be no a priori or preconceived answers to these questions.

Research and the analysis of temporality

What goes for power also goes for the elapsing of time or 'temporality'. In some respects, GT is adept at identifying some of the unfolding 'process' aspects of intersubjective experience – particularly as reflected in concepts such as 'career' (Becker 1953; Stebbins 1970) and/or 'joint activity' (Blumer 1969) (although in a strict sense, since they exist and are known in advance of research, they are 'preconceived' concepts and, as such, do not qualify as 'emergent'). However, more importantly, GT does not attend to time/temporality as it varies within different sectors of social life or its relevance to research questions and problems (Layder 2013). For instance, a person's bodily and biographical time varies considerably, as do personal 'career segments' such as marriage, friendships and work experiences. In turn, in situated activity, time is expressed in the initiation and termination of daily encounters which are, as Goffman (1967) puts it, 'marked by the arrivals and departures' of the participants. Similarly, many types of social setting are characterized by their own 'organizational histories', which differ from the historical time of social systemic phenomena.

Again, IR does not rely on preconceived answers to research questions about temporality 'in advance' of data collection and empirical investigation. The researcher only asks provisional questions in light of his or her knowledge of social domains, their characteristics and properties. From this point onwards, data collection and analysis will provide evidence of the way in which temporality operates in relation to specific research questions and problems.

Using theory in research

GT does not admit the use of concepts from non-GT sources whereas IR actively encourages their use to stimulate the 'emergence' of new concepts and theory. GT dismisses non-GT concepts on the mistaken reasoning that their preconceived nature means that they bear no grounded relation to the empirical world. IR rejects this as an over-generalized critique, even though it is true that *some* types of theory have little connection with empirical evidence. For example, many postmodernists assume that theory bears an uncertain relation to empirical data and evidence. Some 'theorists' deliberately try to destabilize the boundary between fact and fiction under the misguided assumption that this is a step forward. In this regard, they play fast and loose with the distinction between an invented world of theoretical imagination and a real world in which facts and evidence set the terms for theory and explanation. Unfortunately, this fatally undermines the truth-value and credibility of social knowledge and the status of social scientific enquiry. These forms of theorizing are a kind of social 'science fiction' rather than 'social science' with a strong evidential basis.

Of course, there are those who reject the very idea of theory – grounded or otherwise – on the basis that everything about society can be understood in exclusively descriptive and empirical terms. On the other hand, 'anti-theorists' like Becker prefer a more down-to-earth vocabulary, as reflected in his claim that society is really just 'people doing things together' (Becker 1970; see also Bruyn 1966; Rock 1979). From this point of view, there is no need for a conceptual level of analysis abstracted from empirical specifics. Of course, this creates the opposite problem of becoming entrapped in an entirely descriptive and relativistic mode of understanding. It is difficult to construct real explanations of empirical facts/evidence if there are no conceptual/theoretical instruments allowing generalization beyond empirical specifics of time and place.

IR takes a mid-way stance, suggesting that only theory and concepts that engage with the empirical world and social research (including coding, data sampling, data collection and analysis) are able to stimulate novel forms of conceptualization and theorizing. Nevertheless, judging whether theory or concepts are useful to empirical research is not always an easy task (see Chapter 6). However, the central objectives of IR are to encourage conceptual and theoretical innovation in evidence-based research, and to promote research strategies that maximize the synergy between theory and research.

The importance of a literature review

For IR, a literature review is an important means by which the researcher becomes familiarized with the concepts and theoretical ideas that may be of use in a proposed research project, before it is actually begun. By contrast, Glaser (2001) argues against the idea of such a review, on the basis that focusing attention on 'preconceived' ideas and concepts prevents a researcher starting with a clear mind ready to generate novel theory. Instead, the GT researcher should only attend to ideas and concepts that stem directly from immersion in data collection and analysis. Only after theory or concepts have emerged should the researcher consult any existing literature – but only literature that is indicated by the emergent theory. Not all grounded theorists share this view, especially those who espouse a modified, more 'liberal' version of GT and argue for the usefulness of a literature review (Dey 1999; Charmaz 2008). Nevertheless, the original spirit of GT, according to Glaser, is against a literature review at the beginning of a project.

Importantly, IR recommends a 'light-touch' but 'open' literature review that should not be limited to the planning of a project. It should be continuous and regarded as a potential aid throughout a project. In this sense, the continued scanning of relevant literature acts as a focus and reference point for analytical and theoretical reflection on the meaning of incoming data. IR also recommends that initial and ongoing literature reviews – and the reflection and dialogue they promote – are guided and shaped by core research problems and research questions (Layder 2013).

The use of orienting concepts

Being open to a wide range of types of concept and theory, IR favours the use of orienting concepts to help set up initial research designs and sensitize the researcher to relevancies in the data. In essence, this is what an initial literature review seeks to do – to identify appropriate orienting concepts. The crucial proviso about orienting concepts is that although they sensitize and orient, they should not be considered 'sacrosanct' or regarded as permanent fixtures of the structure and design of the project. To varying degrees, both concepts and designs may flexibly change as a result of subsequent data collection and analysis. The use of orienting concepts does not prevent or preclude openness to the influence of 'data disclosures' throughout the research as a whole. In this respect, the investigative approach is as anchored and responsive to data as GT. The crucial difference is that GT put all its eggs into the basket of data disclosure, and thus is exclusively preoccupied with emergent theory and concepts. By contrast, IR reaches towards a judicious blend of 'prior' or 'extant' orienting concepts, bearing in mind their possible modification, elaboration or rejection, as a flexible response to data collection and analysis.

Open-coding and data collection

There are two variants of the GT attitude towards the open-coding of research data. From the 'original' GT point of view, Glaser counsels against too much 'open' or 'line-by-line' coding (of a transcribed interview, say), partly because it generates too many codes, most of which may be of little use further down the line, and partly because it diverts attention away from the more important issue of data analysis and writing 'theoretical memos' which 'help' core categories and concepts to 'emerge' from the data. An alternative view is that open or 'line-by-line' coding (Strauss 1987; Strauss and Corbin 1990) is fine as it offers a very concentrated data analysis and the more codes generated the better, since this increases the number of relevant factors, phenomena or 'variables' to be taken into account.

I side with Glaser's view, although not for the same reasons. True enough, open-coding creates too many codes and encourages the over-accumulation of data, which frequently turns out to be much less important than first thought. Too much data causes confusion in the minds of researchers. Instead, IR focuses on defining and refining the research problem and a set of core questions. This is facilitated both by a continuous 'light-touch' (or less than exhaustive) literature review and the ongoing development of theoretical ideas through the use of orienting concepts. Open coding is jettisoned in favour of 'focused coding', albeit sometimes by the use of provisional 'orienting' concepts. This, however, does not exclude the development of emergent concepts from ongoing data collection and analysis. In fact, it facilitates conceptual development by ensuring that concepts are robust and relate to a wider framework of cumulative knowledge and findings. Codes and coding frames also develop and adapt flexibly in conjunction with orienting concepts as they are confirmed, supported or modified during the project.

Data sampling

In Glaser's original version of GT, the primary and distinctive form of data sampling is 'theoretical' sampling, whereby the researcher continually samples people, events and sites (locations) in terms of the emerging grounded theory yielded by ongoing data analysis. Thus, sampling continually changes emphasis as new sites, events and people are found to be relevant. As more properties of concepts are found and conceptual saturation occurs, the emerging grounded theory absorbs and incorporates them.

In contrast, IR starts on the basis of a more theoretically informed stance because it includes, rather than edits out, a wider range of theoretical influences and resources (extant concepts and theories). In this sense, the notion of 'theoretical' sampling in grounded theory is something of a misnomer for the only theory involved is that which emerges from the current research, or from other *bona fide* grounded theories – those using 'strict' GT methods and rules of procedure. IR not only draws from a vastly wider range of (selectively chosen) potential concepts and theoretical inputs, it also ensures that initial research designs are theoretically informed by social scientific issues beyond the circumscribed remit of GT. Thus, in IR research, problems and questions are also informed by the ontological and epistemological issues (especially those underpinning the social domains model).

In IR, sampling proceeds not only in anticipation of finding emergent concepts and data, but also by developing extant theory and concepts. The synergy between the two ensures that the resulting conceptual innovation derives from a much richer and more inclusive amalgam of influences. In this respect, 'data sampling' – choosing which people, events sites or texts are to be studied, interviewed, observed or interpreted – may be organized in terms of 'behavioural', 'action', 'system', and 'bridging' concepts and their properties.

DIFFERENT UNFOLDING STRATEGIES

The previous points constitute some of the basic differences between GT and IR, although it is worth noting that they ensure that most other aspects of the research process are also very different. Thus, there are fundamental divergences when it comes to: the writing and construction of research proposals; the planning and definition of research designs; the use of research logs (as opposed to diaries or memos); research-writing habits; and the writing up of research reports. (Many of these are covered in Layder (2013), although they are not always directly compared with GT.)

DATA, CONCEPTS AND THEORETICAL DISCOVERY

A superficial grasp of IR might lead the unwary reader to imagine that it closes the door on conceptual innovation. On the surface, it might seem to deny some assumptions that are necessary for researchers to produce novel theory or concepts while remaining 'immersed' in data and its analysis. For example, such an assumption is that theory must remain continuously grounded in data so that it is never too abstract or remote from empirical facts, data or evidence. A related assumption is that researchers must not 'impose' or 'force' concepts or theory on data, but remain 'open' to the meanings of incoming data. IR is entirely in tune with these assumptions but, importantly, it leaves room for a more inclusive view of conceptual and theoretical innovation than in GT. IR underlines the importance of the empirical (or evidential) 'anchoring' of concepts and theory, and although it encourages the use of extant theory and concepts, they are required to have strong links with empirical evidence. In this respect, a number of conditions must be satisfied:

- Extant concepts must be sufficiently specific. They must not be too general or abstract and should have clear referents in the empirical world. That is, they must be able to pinpoint with some precision the kind of data that would count as evidence of their existence.
- Extant concepts must be applicable outside their originating (or 'home') discourse (a network of concepts or a theoretical framework). Furthermore, they must be capable of assimilating with emergent concepts and data from the current project. Concepts from 'master' or 'total' frameworks are often incapable of such assimilation, and are thus not recommended (see Chapter 6).
- To an important extent both the cognitive and substantive validity of concepts depends on supportive evidence. While concepts help to explain the empirical data, data must, in an important sense, underpin their verification. Unless evidence strongly supports concepts, then their validity and adequacy remain questionable.
- Extant concepts must never be 'imposed' or 'forced' on data. Their usefulness depends on their explanatory potential and the extent to which they accord or concur with empirical evidence.
- These 'conditions' allow for a spectrum of types of concept. At one end, there are those that are more or less 'ready-made', but are refined, modified or elaborated via comparison against incoming research data or evidence. At the other end of the spectrum are concepts 'produced' by this dialogical confrontation which do not resemble existing concepts, but which add to or complement them.

CONCEPTUAL GENERATION AND THEORETICAL DISCOVERY

Glaser (2001: 67) speaks of the importance of the researcher obtaining and maintaining a state of mind, which he refers to as 'not knowing', in order to be as receptive as possible to the theoretical possibilities inherent in research data. To be in this state, the researcher must clear his or her mind of all 'existing' preconceived ideas, concepts and theoretical answers to the questions that are posed in the project. From an IR point of view, it is crucial to avoid automatic assumptions about the relevance and fit (validity) of existing theory and concepts. But this is a far cry from dismissing all general theory on the equally automatic assumption that it must be irrelevant or inapplicable. IR regards this as a waste of good theory and concepts that could be derived from a 'light-touch' literature review. It is absolutely necessary to work with received concepts if social research and social science are to benefit in an overall sense. Genuinely cumulative knowledge can only be achieved if extant concepts and knowledge are included in the exercise. Furthermore, if handled carefully and sensitively, the use of preconceived, received or 'already known' concepts certainly does not block the generation of new concepts or theory. In fact, it may facilitate it.

For IR, it is mistaken to believe (as GT suggests) that concepts are generated out of 'pristine' data, coupled with a state of 'not knowing', in advance of data collection and analysis. Such a view invokes the rather mystical idea that data/evidence/empirical facts are capable of 'suggesting' concepts and categories to the researcher, simply by being close to these data. But this overlooks the prior contents of (the researcher's) consciousness, such as common-sense assumptions and understandings, learnt vocabularies, memories of previous research, novels, films, internet searches, newspapers, magazines, comics, and so on.

The thrust of IR helps the researcher adopt a simultaneous 'knowing' and 'not-knowing' attitude without undermining openness to concepts emerging from data collection and analysis. Thus, IR possesses many 'known' features, such as a multidimensional model of social reality, which feed into structured research designs, methodological strategies, the use of orienting concepts, structured coding and sampling frames, and so forth. However, they are tempered by unknowns, such as adaptive responses to data analysis. Thus, IR incorporates 'not knowing' and 'knowing' within the same strategic outlook. The researcher is encouraged to adopt an open-minded approach that also acknowledges the 'known', in terms of previous knowledge and research findings, extant theory and concepts, literature searches and everyday common-sense language (words and concepts).

IR therefore opposes Glaser's claim that 'extant theory is preconceived speculation about answers to research questions and why the answer is correct' (Glaser 2001: 83). It may be that some researchers use extant theory in this manner, particularly those applying some 'grand narrative' or 'master framework' which, in effect, are exercises in self-confirmation by forcing or imposing concepts on data. However, such a 'negative' use of extant theory is by no means inevitable. IR employs extant theory mainly in the form of 'orienting concepts' as initial feeders for theory-generation. The point is to assess the potential usefulness of particular concepts for the explanation of data – in other words, providing answers to research questions and problems.

However, there is no presumption that these concepts are, or will provide, the 'correct answer'. IR merely assumes that particular orienting concepts may be useful starting points from which to investigate and explore research questions. Equally, it may turn out that an orienting concept is not right and that other concepts offer more penetrating insights.

Of course, close contact with incoming data is an important conditioning factor. It encourages researchers to think through potential answers in relation to data. But the data – simply and solely the data – do not, and cannot, suggest concepts or theory independently of the researcher's cognition. Such a cognitive intervention requires some 'imposition' (in a lighter, softer sense) of preconceived thought processes. The 'unsullied' meaning of data does not magically import itself into the researcher's brain. The data are absorbed into the researcher's consciousness via the filter of his or her prior knowledge (including conceptual categories and vocabulary items), which accumulates in a person's brain over time, via psychobiographical experiences.

THE CUL-DE-SAC OF NOT-KNOWING

Glaser's idea that the researcher should somehow contrive to create a 'confusion from not knowing' (2001: 85), in order to be able to generate grounded theory proper, is full of difficulties. For example, it is not at all clear how this 'not knowing' can be achieved. How do you divest your mind of its preconceptions or 'prior' knowledge? How do you become unaware of what you are already aware of? Is this state of affairs possible to achieve in any definable or reliable manner? How can a researcher check whether it has been achieved? Notwithstanding such 'practical' problems, there also remain formidable doubts about the desirability and efficacy of creating 'confusion from not knowing' as a research tactic.

Consciously and regularly eliciting 'confusion from not knowing' (or pretending that you 'have no preconceptions') is likely to lead to more and more confusion about the meanings and possible explanations of data. What is to halt the process of confusion once started? There is certainly no guarantee that close contact with data will ensure that confused 'not-knowing' will somehow be immaculately transformed into theory-generation! With IR, the important question is how to prevent or dispel confusion and anxiety about 'not knowing' and the consequent 'analysis paralysis' so created. The only way of doing this is at some point to *impose* some order on the data. It is an illusion to think that the data themselves suggest and impose this order on the researcher's mind – although this is what GT asks us to believe. But this is to imagine that data have a life of their own – that they somehow dictate or 'call out their own name, or names' as concepts. Data alone cannot install themselves in a researcher's awareness in the form of concepts and theory.

The researcher's (already formed) conceptual vocabulary plays a major role in creating new ways of perceiving and knowing.

With IR, the researcher must abandon any trust in the reliability of 'not-knowing', and face up to the fact that conceptual impositions are necessary to create order in the first place. Thus, there must be a judicious blend of knowing and not knowing in order to benefit from their synergy. Importantly, it is not 'confusion' that must be created or maintained. Rather, it is the discipline of *refusing to impose premature closure* on the creative conceptual solutions that emerge as researchers sort through their preconceptions about the world, and the data that result. If you habitually try to simulate 'not knowing', the resulting confusion will remain and continue until you place your experience – of data, evidence, empirical facts – in the context of some (conceptual) framework in which they make sense.

DISCOVERY OR INNOVATION?

In sum, IR takes a more open and inclusive stance than GT on emergent concepts and theory. New concepts are not directly 'suggested' by data, neither do they emerge simply and solely from data analysis. Rather, concepts are forged out of a response to an 'absence' or 'lack' in an existing (theoretical or descriptive) vocabulary. In this sense, all concepts, whether emergent or received, cannot be divorced from pre-existing networks (of concepts) in which they are semantically embedded, and from which they derive at least some of their overall meaning in relation to data. IR rests on the assumption that concepts 'emerge' from empirical research only as a specific outcome of the synergy between three factors.

First, concepts must be continually monitored in relation to incoming data so that the researcher is able to assess the 'closeness of fit' between them and their empirical indicator(s). Second, 'emergent' concepts must be assessed in relation to other (extant) concepts in their embedding networks, as to whether they offer the best explanation or interpretation of the data in question. Third, the researcher's task in data analysis is to combine the partly separable influences of these two processes. In this sense, it is more accurate to think of emergent concepts as innovative products of rational (or ideational) elements as they confront empirical inputs, rather than as items of 'pure' empirical 'discovery'. Concepts never simply emerge from unfettered data analysis. They are always worked on, and through the researcher's existing vocabulary of concepts. The investigative approach thus avoids the pitfalls of empiricism that haunt GT and limit its explanatory power.

Because of GT's flat and monochrome ontology – its model or image of social reality – it is limited to the use and 'discovery' of 'behavioural' concepts, those tied to the domain of situated activity (or what Goffman (1983) refers to as 'the interaction order').

In contrast, IR embraces a much wider array of types of concept and theory, which represent and reflect multiple domains and bring together subjective (agency) and objective (system) aspects of social life. There is no doubt that behavioural concepts are massively important, but IR also includes 'structural' or 'systemic' concepts as well as 'bridging' concepts, which offer a more subtle and complex understanding of behaviour and situated activity. Since, in GT's model, social reality is compacted and contained within the interactive, interpersonal sphere (the 'participant's concerns', in Glaser's terms), it does not include, nor is it capable of generating, concepts which capture or reflect the ontological variegation of social life. The model of social reality that underpins IR allows for a greater range (and explanatory power) of concepts generated during data analysis. In the process, it also encourages the use of a wide range of 'received' or 'extant' concepts in empirical research.

GROUNDED THEORY MARK 2: ONE STEP FORWARD AND THREE BACK?

I have referred to Charmaz's 'revised' version of GT in the discussion of power. Here I want to consider her claim to have developed a radically more advanced version of GT in terms of '21st century constructivism' (Charmaz 2008). By proclaiming the birth of 'constructivist GT', Charmaz sharply distinguishes it from what she defines as Glaser's 'objectivist' version, disparaging the weaknesses of the latter while retaining Glaser and Strauss's original label of 'grounded theory' (Glaser and Strauss's original title). I have already identified some formidable weaknesses of Glaser's GT. Here I want to challenge Charmaz's claim to have advanced beyond Glaser's version in anything but fairly superficial ways. In essence, I argue that her constructivist version occupies exactly the same epistemological and ontological ground as Glaser's GT, and because her version is subject to the same limitations, it fails to resolve any of its basic problems.

The myth of Glaser's objectivism

Charmaz creates the 'illusion' of difference between her own and Glaser's versions of GT by indulging in some relabelling and redefinition. Thus, her 'constructivist' version is counterposed to what she claims is Glaser's 'objectivist' version. This labelling of Glaser's GT conveniently plays into the sympathies of those who already accept some of the naïveties of postmodernism but, more importantly, it is also a misleading characterization of Glaser's GT. The relabelling creates the impression that because she is the 'constructivist' and Glaser the 'objectivist', it follows that he does not, in any sense, share any part of her constructivist epistemology or ontology. This latter is an inaccurate reading of Glaser's position because in fact he shares (along with other inter-actionists and phenomenologists) many of her assumptions about the nature of social reality, social analysis and social research.

Even as a stringent critic of Glaser, I would argue that it is just not true to say that he is an 'objectivist' on the basis that he only seeks 'explanation and prediction at a general level abstracted from the specific research site and process', and that by comparison 'social constructionists are able to move from local worlds to a more general conceptual level' (Charmaz 2008: 398). Glaser and Strauss's very important and central distinction between 'substantive' and 'formal' theory is designed to do just this, to move between local and general levels of analysis. This 'capability' is not unique to social constructionists either, as Charmaz implies. For example, investigative research is not, in the remotest sense, based on social constructionist principles or assumptions, and yet one of its central features is a constant tacking 'to and fro' between general and specific (or local) levels, as a result of its two-tier approach – the social domains model yoked to a data-gathering project.

The actual situation is the exact opposite of what Charmaz claims it to be. In fact, 'social constructionism' is unable to properly engage with a more general (conceptual and abstract) level of analysis. It cannot tack between local and general levels because it is obsessively tied to documenting the endless self-reflexive process in which researchers and participants co-construct the research itself. Social constructionism is trapped within its own local microcosm of self-reflexivity and cannot rise above the 'co-constructed' viewpoints of researchers and/or participants. As a result, social constructionism deflects attention away from the original point and content of research, which is to explain naturally occurring social behaviour. Instead, the methods focus is on researcher's reflexive abilities, and their co-construction of the research process (with the research participants), while the 'original' research problem, its subject matter or topic, is neatly placed to one side. The problem that originally prompted the research is bracketed-out, while the research findings, explanations and conclusions become absorbed into the documentation of the research process. Taken to its extreme, constructionist research becomes an intense but fairly vacuous scrutiny of the research process itself, rather than an attempt to analytically grasp or explain its original problem (subject matter or topic).

The myth of a single objective reality and of passive observers

Charmaz takes a rather simplistic 'straw-man' view of 'objectivism' in asserting that it 'assumes a single reality that a passive neutral observer discovers through value-free inquiry' and that this makes 'data selection, collection and representation unproblematic; they become *givens* rather than *constructions* that occur during the research process and shape its outcome' (Charmaz 2008: 401–2, my emphasis.) First, it is not necessary to 'assume a single reality' in order to acknowledge 'objective' elements of social reality. There may be many (different) objective features of reality, and indeed there are multiple objective realities within the social world – although not an indefinite number. In this sense 'social domains' represent the variegated entangled realities that constitute the social world. Acknowledging the objective moments of social reality does not require a belief in a single reality.

The same is true of the claim that objectivism assumes a 'passive neutral observer who discovers the single reality through value-free inquiry'. In fact, this is a nonsensical claim – even when applied to the stereotypical 'positivist social scientist' it is meant to depict. Just think about it. If researchers were, in fact, 'passive, neutral and value-free', then they would be akin to mindless robots incapable of making any autonomous decisions at all, let alone conducting something as complicated as social research. The best such a researcher could do would be to stare emptily into space! Indeed, for a researcher to appreciate the objective facets of social life, she or he must embrace specific values and practices. Perhaps the most important of these is to be able to distance her or his self from the (co-construction of the) research process, enough to disentangle the personal preconceptions, prejudgements and reflexive blinkers that might get in the way of coming to grips with the subject matter and problem-focus of the research. Equally, the moderate objectivist *would not assume* that data selection, collection and representation are unproblematic. It may be that she or he would consider different sorts of things problematic, as compared with a constructivist researcher who focuses on the process of co-construction itself.

CONSTRUCTIONIST GROUNDED THEORY: AN EVEN MORE LIMITED VERSION?

Charmaz's overall position rejects the existence of any partly independent objective or subjective elements in the social world. Social reality is nothing other than eternal co-construction through inter-subjective activity. Social patterns, organization, macro phenomena, social system aspects, forms of domination and historical products have no properties or emergent characteristics distinct from situated social encounters. For constructionists, there is nothing other than inter-subjectivity, memory, consciousness and local practices.

In this sense, the constructionist strategy is rather like building a room/shelter, sealing the entrance, trapping oneself inside and then claiming that nothing exists beyond its confines. The 'trapped' constructionist cannot envision the wider environment in which its 'shelter' of assumptions is embedded. But there is no reason to limit social research in this manner. Social research benefits immeasurably from conceiving of social reality as a complex intertwining of subjective, inter-subjective and objective elements. In this respect, Charmaz's social constructionism does not expand or open up Glaser's GT. In fact, it simply offers an even more inward-looking version of much the same approach. At least (according to Charmaz) Glaser is 'aware' of objective elements of reality in his recognition of the need to generalize from local (research site) co-constructions in order to produce findings of relevance beyond them. In this sense, Glaser's GT is not constricted in the way Charmaz's is, by her extreme constructivist emphasis. At the same time, her version of GT shares a similar 'flat' model of social reality, which eliminates partly independent subjective and objective elements.

At this point Charmaz's claimed 'consistency' with Marx's ideas and the Marxist view of history is strained to the point of collapse. Her strategy is to offer some basic Marxian ideas and, without supporting argument or justification, simply assert that they are consistent with social constructionism. For example, she says, 'consistent with Marx I assume that people make their worlds but do not make them as they please. Rather, worlds are constructed under particular historical and social conditions that shape our views, actions and collective practices' (Charmaz 2008: 409, note 2). And again, 'I come close to the Marxist view of history ... because I acknowledge human agency but assert that it always occurs within a pre-existing social frame with its constraints – of which we may be unaware and which may not be of our own choosing' (2008: 409, note 8). Obviously, these are Marx's ideas, but Charmaz does not appreciate or analyse their implications, nor come anywhere near to demonstrating epistemologically or ontologically that they are consistent with constructionism.

This is clear if we examine Marx and Engels' famous statement that people do not make history 'under circumstances chosen by themselves but under circumstances directly encountered, given and transmitted from the past. The tradition of all the dead generations weighs like a nightmare on the brain of the living' (Marx and Engels 1968: 96). Charmaz fails to recognize the implications of this last sentence. She does not ask why the 'tradition of all the dead generations weigh like a nightmare on the brain of the living'? The answer is because the 'living' have no choice about the social conditions of existence that the 'dead generations' have bequeathed to them in the form of the capitalist system. Capitalism is an unequal system of economic and social relations of production, power, domination and relations of ruling, reproduced over historical time. It is precisely these 'objective' (pre-given) features which limit, shape and constrain the capacities of the living to 'construct' (or co-construct') their everyday realities. Further, it is precisely these phenomena that constructionism is unable to analyse, or research, because its ontology (model of reality) is limited to the domain of situated co-construction. It has no analytical means of grasping the 'systemic' elements of society (capitalism) in which the social conditions of the living are the (relatively) objective products of past (dead) generations, and which exert constraints on actions, values and life chances.

Charmaz acknowledges the existence of constraints but doesn't analyse their nature. Crucially, she does not show how *constraints limit the co-constructive capacities of researchers or participants*. Constraints do not play a role in constructivist data analysis and research. I discuss some of the practical implications of this for coding, data sampling and concept formation at the end of the chapter. By contrast, in IR constraints (and enablements) are factored into research via the analysis of social settings and contextual resources. In this manner, the domains model avoids the reductionist flat ontology of constructionism, making possible a richer and more nuanced approach to empirical investigation.

In this sense, Charmaz's belief that she has gone beyond the limitations of Glaser's version of GT, such as by allowing an apparently wider openness to theories, is undercut by the fact that all versions of GT are hemmed-in by their highly constricted model of social reality, which disallows objective or subjective elements. This enforces a limited range of 'admissible' or 'appropriate' forms of theory, concepts and analysis. In this sense, it is absolutely not true, as Charmaz claims, 'that as a method for studying social processes', GT 'can be adopted by researchers who hold different theoretical perspectives, focus on various levels of analysis, and 'pursue varied objectives' (Charmaz 2012: 1–2). As the discussion below of practical methods and issues shows, GT *is incompatible* with many perspectives, levels of analysis and objectives.

For instance, GT's premises and assumptions would not permit or even nominally support an approach like investigative research, which is based on and shaped around a variegated model of social reality – multiple social domains – with intertwining links between subjective, inter-subjective and objective social phenomena. To support such a model and approach would be impossible in terms of the flat, constructionist model with its black hole of inter-subjectivity. This is not only about 'big' or fundamental issues or differences in epistemology and ontology. Crucial differences in research practice, such as data gathering, sampling, coding and concept-formation, emerge as a result of the fundamental constrictions of Charmaz's constructionist GT.

PRACTICAL LIMITATIONS OF CONSTRUCTIONIST GROUNDED THEORY

Many researchers believe that research is simply about deciding on the best ways of gaining access to, and collecting, facts, information, data and evidence. But this is a major error. What is defined as, and what in research terms count as, *relevant* facts, information data and evidence are very much influenced by less 'obvious' – and deeper – issues of approach and principle. Emphatically, this is not to say that such deeper issues *entirely determine* what we believe to be the facts, data, evidence and information. The latter always have some degree of 'independence' in this respect. However, it is of critical importance to be aware of the role they do play in defining the things we treat as evidence, and generally characterizing the topics or problems that we investigate, in order that we factor them into our research preparations, strategies and findings. These considerations are illustrated in some of the practical implications of the differences between GT and IR.

Coding

Coding is the process by which a researcher assigns a 'code' or 'label' to a block or sequence of data, such as an extract from an interview transcript or a quotation from a document (book, newspaper, email), or observations or documents (photographs, paintings). Coding allows the researcher to break up the data in terms of categories, making them more easily understandable and 'analysable' in relation to research problems and core questions. Charmaz (2012: 5) suggests that for her version of GT it is best to code data in terms of 'processes actions and meanings'. Examples, of such codes in relation to medical research would be:

> 'Being sent away'.
>
> 'Getting a bad doctor'.
>
> 'Being admitted to hospital'. (Charmaz 2012: 7)
>
> On the other hand, according to Charmaz, most qualitative researchers code for 'topics' and 'themes'. Equivalent examples would be:
>
> 'Hospitalization'.
>
> 'Conflict with doctor'.
>
> 'Physician control'. (Charmaz 2012: 6)

Charmaz argues that coding for actions and meanings allows the researcher to see 'much more' in the data, and that it is uniquely suited to 'defining connections between data' and 'analysing' rather than 'describing' them. I disagree with Charmaz in relation to all these claims. Rather than allowing the researcher to 'see more' in data, coding exclusively in terms of action and meanings forces the researcher to narrow the potential focus on relevant social phenomena. Second, this type of coding is no more suited to defining connections in data than coding for 'topics' and 'themes'. Finally, coding for action and meaning is skewed towards description rather than analysis, because the latter requires a broader and more penetrating perspective.

Why restrict coding in this manner?

Coding for 'action and meanings' or, in other words, things relevant to 'the doing and being of actors' (their existential situation) imposes a severe restriction on what is relevant in social life generally, and relevant for research purposes in particular. It also artificially limits the factors crucial to explaining social behaviour, research problems and research questions.

Charmaz's perspective on coding omits social processes and phenomena that are not simply present in people's actions and meanings (and cannot be read-off from them). For example, action and meaning depend on, and are influenced by, the settings and wider societal contexts in which they are embedded. Coding, for example, may valuably be around 'social settings' (such as labour markets) and formal organizations (such as hospitals, factories, universities, schools, stock markets, financial institutions), and include the appraisal systems, status and authority hierarchies, and so forth, embodied in them. Coding can also profitably be around 'contextual resources', such as class, ethnicity, gender or social media influences (on values, habits and tastes). 'Settings' and 'contextual resources' are not reducible to, and cannot necessarily be discerned in, or deduced from, participants' own accounts (of their actions and meanings). System phenomena have properties which constrain or otherwise shape actions and meaning. Codes around them would be entirely missing from Charmaz's scenario. Examples of codes for settings might be:

'Career appraisal systems'.

'Segmented labour markets'.

'Open or sheltered labour markets'.

'Hierarchical or flat authority and status systems'.

'Situational and positional authority/power'.

Examples of codes around 'contextual resources' might include:

'Class or gender background, poverty/inequality'.

'Cultural milieu: habits and values'.

'Aesthetics, fashion and taste'.

'Consumer habits, life chances, spending power'.

It is important to code such systemic phenomena independently of actions and meanings since they have characteristics that are not necessarily transparent in people's actions or their reflections about 'what is going on' in their lived, experienced worlds. Coding entirely for action and meaning will exclude systemic phenomena which significantly influence the manner in which actions and meaning are formed and shaped.

What about coding for psychobiographical processes? Following Charmaz's advice would mean excluding such 'unimportant' subjective factors. Processes of psychological influence would not be coded and their significance would be lost to the research. Examples of codes and coding around psychobiographical issues might include:

'Personal resilience'.

'Fear of intimacy'.

'Level of security/insecurity, confidence or self-esteem'.

'Personal skills, benign power, personal efficacy, depression'.

'Self-estrangement, feelings of unreality'.

'Preferences, tastes, beliefs, obsessions, anxieties'.

Coding along these dimensions is essential in IR, although not necessarily at the same time. Restricting coding to participants' 'actions and meanings' distorts out of all proportion their overall importance for explaining social processes and behaviour. In this sense, Charmaz's claim that her version of GT facilitates analysis rather than description is misleading because it depends on accepting that 'analysis', in this sense, would mean a less than full explanation of social behaviour. A full explanation would require a broader examination of how 'action and meaning' emerge from multiple domain influences.

Concept-formation

In IR, codes and the process of coding data are intimately related to concept-formation and theory-generation. Codes are provisional ways of understanding how data contribute to the overall explanation of behaviour. An important distinction is that between 'member defined' (or 'in vivo') codes and concepts, as compared with those that are 'researcher-defined'. The distinction is not hard and fast in that sometimes researchers rely on participants' or members' accounts slightly more than their own, while in other cases they rely on their own perceptions to inform codes and concepts. With the latter, researchers draw upon their accumulated research experience and their knowledge of published findings in order to come up with conceptual representations of behaviour. In this sense, the use of researcher-defined codes and concepts (and the constant interchange with 'in vivo' types) establishes an essential link between empirical research and a body of extant material and knowledge (facts, concepts, theories findings) from previous generations of researchers. This link provides an assurance that IR findings are not limited by an empiricist theory of knowledge. By contrast, such empiricist limitations are a natural consequence of restricting codes and concepts to action and meaning.

This issue relates back to a point made earlier in the chapter in relation to GT more generally. That is, the gaps between GT and IR are not simply reflected in the vast differences between their respective models of social reality, but also in terms of their epistemological assumptions. Investigative research counters empiricism by acknowledging that some domains of reality require types of concept other than those relevant to inter-subjective reality. In IR, the latter are referred to as:

'Action or behavioural concepts' depicting the 'experienced', 'lived' world – the existential core of social life – are pivotally important to a comprehensive explanation of social behaviour. They give rise to sub-codes and concepts such as 'dynamics of interpersonal influence' or 'strategies of manipulation', both of which indicate aspects of interpersonal power. Such concepts do not simply represent action and meaning from participants' viewpoints. They have a somewhat 'objective' cast to them, in that they refer to action and meaning from a more impersonal, analytical standpoint and are derived from accumulated research knowledge. Nonetheless, they are crucial for laying the conceptual foundations of a robust, non-empiricist explanation of behaviour, one that includes, but is not limited to or by, participant accounts.

For IR, action or behavioural concepts do not exhaust conceptual possibilities, thus there are multiple types of concept reflecting the specific properties of different domains of social reality. Action concepts themselves can therefore be subdivided between those relevant to situated activity (or interpersonal encounters) and those identifying more subjective aspects, such as individual skills and predispositions.

'Psychobiographical concepts' thus refer to individuals' skills, feelings, preferences, likes, dislikes, personal powers of persuasion, benign manipulation, intimacy, and so on. That is, those individual attributes and personality characteristics that feed directly into interactive situations and interpersonal encounters but whose relatively independent influences and effects remain unacknowledged in a social constructionist perspective.

If the above types of concept refer to aspects of the life-world, then others refer to system aspects of the social world. There are two sub-types.

'Concepts pertinent to social settings' pinpoint the properties of different kinds of settings. Thus, for example, 'positional power and authority' are pertinent to formally patterned settings such as work organizations (public, private or commercial) as are 'hierarchical' versus 'egalitarian, status systems'. Concepts indicating informal status and/or 'leadership' characteristics are relevant to less formal settings, such as families, gangs, terrorist groups, or those to do with sexual and romantic intimacy.

'Concepts around contextual resources' mainly refer to the consequences of structural or systemic power and how it generates unequal access to, and distribution of, economic and cultural resources along divisions of class, gender, ethnicity and age.

Finally, there are *'bridging concepts'*, which forge connections across the life-world–system boundary. Such concepts often spotlight social processes at the intersection between situated activity and settings, since they congregate along the life-world–system boundary. Bridging concepts have a dual nature – a psychological component fused with a social relational component. Good examples are 'alienated' or 'calculative' involvement and/or commitment of people or workers or employees in factories or administrative organizations.

CODING, CONCEPT-FORMATION AND SAMPLING IN INVESTIGATIVE RESEARCH

Clearly, GT cannot tolerate or sustain such concepts in terms of its knowledge basis (epistemology) and reality assumptions (its model or vision of reality). But for IR, its array of concept types reflecting different facets of social reality are necessary in order to develop comprehensive (rather than incomplete) explanations of research topics and problems. Their existence allows IR to establish logical and practical connections between coding, concept-formation and sampling as research proceeds. Thus, while the research might have begun with an initial sample, it might be added to or elaborated by seeking new categories or types of interviewee or informant as a result of the ongoing development of concepts. In this sense, continuous 'conceptual sampling' (featuring all the types) becomes a possibility for IR whereas for GT (constructionist or otherwise) it would be outlawed.

5

THE ARC OF INVESTIGATIVE RESEARCH

CHAPTER CONTENTS

This chapter presents a systematic overview of the investigative research approach and highlights its distinctive features. IR is not designed to be cut entirely adrift from alternative approaches, so as far as possible I press home the importance of convergences and overlaps with other research approaches. By and large, I have sidelined issues around research ethics. This is partly because more specialized and detailed treatments of such issues can be found elsewhere. But emphatically, this is not because they are any less important for IR than for other approaches. In this regard, the following ethical principles are integral to IR, as they are to all other forms of research: 'informed consent' (and the varieties thereof); the protection of participants from harm and deception and to guard their interests; the protection of vulnerable subjects; and issues of the 'confidentially' and 'anonymity' of research subjects. It is because such ethical issues are relevant and common to all forms of social research that they have no extra or specific role to play in IR.

On the other hand, issues of validity are integral to IR in ways that often do not apply to other approaches. As a result, in what follows I show how they relate to particular segments or phases of IR. The IR process itself is accurately characterized as 'problem-driven', and while other approaches make similar claims, what they mean by this is usually quite different. In this sense, validity issues are 'front-loaded' and ramify throughout the whole research process. They must not be treated as separate or discrete issues relevant only to particular phases (or stages) of research.

THE RESEARCH ARC: PHASES AND CYCLES

The six-phase sequence described below represents one completed cycle of the IR research process. Often, both in principle and in practice, the cycle may be repeated several times (in abbreviated form) in order for the full effects to take hold. The number of cycles (or half-cycles) actually required will depend on factors specific to the project in question. It is best to maintain flexibility about this since while most projects require several cycles and phases, it is possible that one cycle – the first – might represent the entire project, from beginning to end. As depicted below, the sequence of phases represents the complete research process, although in practice researchers are free to employ various abbreviated 'mini-cycles'.

MODELS OF THE RESEARCH PROCESS

To situate IR in relation to other models of the research process it is useful to refer to Punch's continuum between 'pre-specified' (tight or pre-planned) versus 'unfolding' (or loose) models (Punch 2008). Punch points out that the essential difference between them is

> about when in the research process structure is introduced. The structure can be introduced in the planning or pre-empirical stage, when the research is being set up, before data are collected; or, it can be introduced in the execution stage of the research, as the study is being carried out, as data are being collected. (Punch 2008: 24)

Quantitative research based on surveys and experimental studies typically falls towards the pre-specified end of the continuum. Specific research questions and conceptual frameworks are set up in advance to guide the study and the design is tightly structured, requiring that variables are identified and that their conceptual status in the research is made clear. Quantitative data are structured in advance, while measurement also imparts numerical structure to data, and there is an overriding concern with using data as a means of verifying theory (and concepts) (Punch 2008: 22–25).

In contrast, qualitative research (such as case studies and ethnographies, participant observation, GT) typically occupies a much greater range along the continuum, but tends more often to conform to the unfolding mode (Punch 2008: 22). Only general questions are set out in advance of data collection since until some empirical work is carried out, it is not possible to identify specific research questions. 'They will only become clear as the research unfolds and as a specific focus for the work is developed' (Punch 2008: 23). Similarly, concepts and conceptual frameworks can only emerge as the research proceeds and this creates an emphasis on theory-generation. Research design only takes detailed shape as the research progresses and the specific focus is developed. With the unfolding model, data are unstructured at the point of collection and no pre-established categories or codes are used, they emerge from the data during the analysis. Although Punch suggests that qualitative studies occupy a greater range along the 'pre-specified-unfolding' continuum, he also observes that 'many of them' are closer to the unfolding model. In support, he quotes Miles and Huberman's stated preference for 'a more loosely structured, emergent, inductively "grounded" approach to gathering data', in which 'the conceptual framework should emerge from the field during the course of the study' (Miles and Huberman 1994: 17).

AN OVERVIEW OF THE IR MODEL

Punch's 'pre-specified' versus 'unfolding' model (or Miles and Huberman's 'tight' versus 'loose' model) of the research process very usefully draws attention to important general elements applying to many types of research. Several of these elements are incorporated in the IR schema, while many others are not. However, there are two major respects in which the IR version of the research process differs from those of Punch and Miles and Huberman. First, IR is predicated on a multi-strategy approach (Layder 1993) that is open to the use of both quantitative and qualitative methods and data, either as mono-methods or as properly 'integrated' mixtures (taking account of underpinning models of social reality and epistemic premises). But there is no requirement that IR research *must* involve a mixed-methods approach. Second, IR incorporates elements of the 'pre-specified or tight' versus the 'unfolding or loose' models but welds them into an integrated whole in which pre-specified elements are followed by unfolding elements, and then by further pre-specification and more unfolding, and so on. The model depends on the dynamics of iterative cycling, and continuous switching between 'problem-formulation' and 'reformulation' (my alternative terms for 'pre-specified' and 'unfolding').

In the following discussion, all six phases are examined in more detail, while also introducing the important notions of an *explanatory spine* and its close companion, the *integrated chain of reasoning,* that underpins the process as a whole. These two continuously influence the whole span of the research arc, thus keeping emergent concepts recursively tied-in to their evidential basis. Thus, validity and credibility claims infuse IR, particularly through the guiding principle of 'problem relevance' which underlines its problem-driven character.

CYCLE-PHASE DYNAMICS

The first phase of the cycle is concerned with initial problem-formulation and the construction of a preliminary conceptual scaffold. The researcher settles on a problem-focus for the research, along with a corresponding set of research questions and a rudimentary conceptual/theoretical scaffold on which to base a 'projected' explanation of the social behaviour in question. This sets in motion a chain of reasoning that underpins the validity claims of IR (and directly feeds into issues of credibility, plausibility and reliability in relation to data, methods, sampling, coding and analysis).

The cycle moves from formulating an initial problem-focus, along with core research questions and an orienting (conceptual) scaffold, straight through to a research proposal and design. Then come the practical phases, including data sampling, data collection, coding and analysis. In many approaches, this is regarded as the natural end of a project, presaging the announcement of research findings and conclusions. However, with IR this typically signals a fresh round of the cycle. So instead of a 'conclusion', the end of the first cycle is, in fact, a detailed questioning and evaluation of the orienting scaffold. To what extent does it offer an appropriate and robust explanation of the data and evidence so far? If the explanation falls short of these standards and criteria, then the problem-focus must be reformulated, refined or retuned. In turn, such readjustments might precipitate another round of sampling, data collection, coding and analysis in order to develop a more adequate explanation of the data/evidence. Until a satisfactory explanation is reached, the process may be repeated, with each cycle moving successively in and out of this arc or pattern.

FLEXIBLY STRUCTURED ADAPTATION

Returning to Punch's 'pre-specified' and 'unfolding' and Miles and Huberman's 'tight' and 'loose' models of the research process, it is clear that IR conforms *in toto* to neither of the types, but does include some elements of both in a unique combination. A prominent aspect of this is that 'once in play' (once data collection has begun) the tendency and momentum of the cycle is to move back to a pre-specified or tight phase – although transmuted into a new (altered or refined) scaffold and problem focus. An analogy with football might be useful.

Before the start of play a football team always adopts a fixed team pattern or formation and all the individual players occupy their places/positions within it. However, once in play, this formation shifts around as the individual players move into and out of various positions or spaces on the field of play. The original formation segues into mobile, constantly shifting alignments and configurations of players enacting 'team plays'. Once a goal is scored, the players return to their original starting positions to restart the game. So the game always restarts with a pre-specified formation and returns to this same formation at the end of each completed cycle – signalled by a goal being scored. The number of cycles depends on the number of goals scored, which is not predetermined or predictable.

While the process and the unpredictable number of cycles are broadly similar in IR, it differs considerably in other respects. In football, after each completed cycle (a goal) the team always reverts back to the same (pre-specified) formation to restart the play. In IR, however, the end of each cycle returns to a changed formation – in the guise of an orienting scaffold altered in response to data collection and analysis. So, with IR, the iterative cycle (of data collection and analysis) is repeated on the basis of a refashioned orienting scaffold until some overall explanatory schema has fully matured. Thus, the IR model is not continuously 'unfolding' in accordance with one linear path. If anything, it is continuously re-specified and restructured in multiple directions (and cycles). The orienting scaffold and problem-focus are questioned, probed, and eventually 'pressured' into a new formation, to organize and redirect succeeding phases and cycles.

Changes to the orienting scaffold and problem-focus trigger changes in the five succeeding phases. Thus, there may be readjustments to the proposal and design, additions to data samples, a retuning of data collection strategies, and refinements to coding practices and data analysis. Within each phase, the research arc 'unfolds' but only to metamorphose into a newly emergent orienting scaffold. The number of repeated cycles required will depend on such things as research costs, or difficulties in finding and accessing additional sampling units, be they people or physical locales. But it will also depend on the need for an ever more robust explanation to emerge, and this is therefore crucial to determining the length of the overall project. As a general rule, however, two to three cycles will be sufficient.

PROBLEM-FORMULATION AND ORIENTING SCAFFOLD

Research problems and research topics

Research problems are not the same as social problems. Social problems (such as an increase in gun or knife crime, or poverty, or the prevalence of anxiety disorders among teenagers) denote an unsatisfactory state of affairs in society which is deemed by government, interest groups or policy makers to be in need of a solution. In order to research a social problem, it must first be converted into a *researchable* problem. In this regard, it is more productive to think of social problems as research '*topics*' rather than research problems. The questions that flow from research problems are about the operations of society, its networks, social systems and social activities in a general sense. Research topics are more empirically defined and factually delineated, referring to specific activities or sectors of society, such as industry, leisure, sport, welfare, criminal justice, and so on. Further, research problems are more analytical and theoretical in nature, while research topics are more descriptive and information-defined.

Research questions: problem and topic questions

In IR, research is problem-driven, and '*problem questions*' are about the way in which social domains shape and influence social behaviour generally. Examples of problem questions are: How are individual psychobiographies influenced by social involvements over time? How do local interactions produce emergent outcomes? How do social settings influence social activity? In what ways do asymmetric distributions of resources shape social behaviour? How are these questions affected by the passage of time or the influence of different forms of power? As these examples show, problem questions are, to a large extent, general, conceptual, abstract and explanatory. They are concerned with issues applicable across whole classes of empirical phenomena.

Topic questions, on the other hand, describe actual empirical instances of the influence of domains using primarily facts and information. By transposing problem questions into topic questions about drug taking we get the following: Is drug taking the result of individual factors (predispositions, motives)? How do long-term drug users influence new users? To what extent are patterns of drug use shaped by schools, gangs or work environments? Do media representations of drugs influence people's attitudes to them?

Core research questions are always a composite of topic questions, which are mainly descriptive, and problem questions, which are mainly theoretical or explanatory. However, topic questions must be rinsed through the conceptual filter of the problem-focus in order that they feed into core research questions. In so doing, the explanatory spine and its connecting links are not clogged up or overwhelmed by the influence of topic questions. Because of empirical density, topic questions are more numerous, descriptive and detailed than problem questions, which are more general and conceptual in nature.

The conditioning 'filter' of problem questions fine-tunes topic questions and helps align them with the most relevant, and the best quality, data. But the filter also delimits their range and content by weeding out those that do not shed any important or additional light on the research problem. This is important in deciding other questions, such as: At what point is data collection complete? When is it appropriate to stop collecting data? When is the research process at an end?

Constructing an orienting scaffold

A sharply defined research problem and set of core questions will help in constructing an orienting scaffold. An orienting scaffold relies on an orienting concept, or concepts, around which an explanation of the social behaviour in question may be built. These provide the initial seeding for the explanatory spine or narrative of the research which, eventually, will be woven into a series of arguments that attempt to resolve the research problem and answer the core questions. Orienting concepts are essentially 'preliminary' and tentatively advanced as an initial means of sorting and analysing data. As soon as data analysis has begun, the extent of their usefulness or relevance begins to reveal itself more clearly. The selection and choice of potential orienting concepts requires some familiarity with published studies of the problem, area or topic, or more general discussions around the concepts in question. A selective literature review (Layder 2013) facilitates the search for appropriate orienting concepts, which should be chosen for their capacity to guide analysis, not to predetermine or preconceive it. The criteria governing their selection include the following:

1. The concept should have an obvious empirical and analytical relevance to the substantive area or topic in question.
2. Such concepts should reflect or shed light on the causal influence of social domains – that is, their interconnections with social processes involving aspects of agency and structure, subjective–objective features of social life, or macro and micro levels of analysis.

Research proposal and design

Viewed together, a research problem, a core set of questions and an orienting scaffold form a robust, but provisional, launching platform which directly informs the research proposal and design. They enable the researcher to plan in some detail the kind of data that is needed, how to source and collect it, and other broader strategies. A robust proposal and design does not impose a rigidity and fixity upon the overall research plan or the unfolding of the project. IR remains adaptively flexible to changing circumstances, unanticipated data and data collection problems, as well as to the evolution of analytical ideas and concepts. The extent of such changes will largely depend on the internal dynamics of the project and the dialectic between data collection and data analysis.

Data sampling

The sampling phase of the IR cycle concerns decisions about data sources: What sort of people, incidents, observations, documents or texts are needed? What criteria are involved in such decisions? There are several issues that need to be clarified. 'Problem sampling' and 'conceptual sampling' are the default sampling techniques in IR and differ markedly from 'probability' (or random) sampling in quantitative research. They also differ, although less extremely, from 'purposive' or 'strategic' sampling (Patton 2001) in qualitative research.

Problem sampling

Problem sampling relies on data that is representative of the problem-focus of the research and excludes those units not relevant to it. The primary objective is *not* to obtain a representative sample of the larger general population from which it is drawn, as in probability sampling. This is because there is no guarantee that a general (or typical) population will contain instances (of behaviour, events, incidents), that reflect the problem-focus, and thus the chances of their being included in the sample will be very low. Probability sampling cannot efficiently target or capture data or sampling units appropriate or relevant to the problem-focus. Problem sampling places the emphasis on 'problem representativeness' rather 'population representativeness' in order to achieve more control over the relevance of the sampling units.

Probability samples select random samples that permit confident generalization from the sample to the larger population, since every unit in the universe (the population under study) has the same probability of being included or selected in the sample. In problem sampling the sample is chosen on the principle of problem-relevance, and as such permits confident generalization from the sample to a more encompassing, but specific, population, reflecting the analytical and real-life issues associated with a defined problem-focus. It cannot automatically be assumed that a problem-focus will exist in a general population, thus it may not represent a specific problem-focus.

Probability sampling is appropriate to survey analysis or experiments where the researcher is interested in, and exerts a high degree of control over, the quantitative measurement of relations between 'discrete' variables (like educational attainment or socio-economic background). However, as Yin (2009) points out, it is quite inappropriate to apply the logic of probability sampling to types of research over which the investigator has little control, such as real-life events and situations. Similarly, it is not appropriate to research which deals with complex ensembles of social processes and social relations and requires in-depth examination of the interrelationships between social domains.

Problem sampling is much closer to 'purposive' or 'strategic' sampling (Patton 2001), the logic and power of which depends on targeted data and the extraction of information-rich cases for in-depth study. A crucial difference is that in problem sampling, unit selection is limited both by the relevant problem-focus and its pertinence to the explanation of social behaviour – in this case in terms of entangled domains, as below.

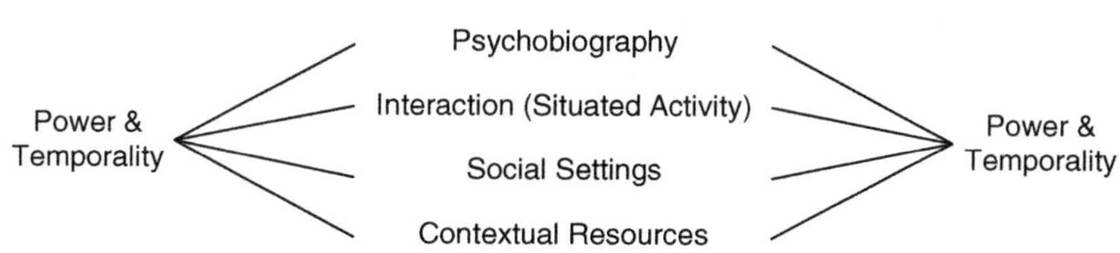

Problem sampling and theory development

IR does not set out to test-out or verify hypotheses about the relations between quantitatively measurable variables. In large part, IR has an *exploratory* remit, investigating issues around problem-foci, rather than a testing agenda. Although elements of testing are part of this remit, as when evaluating orienting concepts against empirical evidence, this is very different from testing hypotheses about relationships between variables. IR is more concerned with generating innovative analytical ideas and encouraging theory-development and concept-generation. Such an emphasis demands a flexibility in research designs and sampling frames that is not possible in 'variable' research such as surveys and experiments. While this is closer to the unfolding designs of much qualitative research, there are also pronounced differences. IR is much more inclusive with regard to a diversity of forms of theory (including general theory and middle-range theory) and more positive about their potential for research, while at the same time not endorsing all forms of theory and theorizing. In fact, it rejects laissez-faire eclecticism, or the abandonment of scientific principles. Theory must be empirically anchored and rigorously reasoned, but not imposed as an overarching theoretical lens or perspective.

It follows that IR is also at odds with those qualitative approaches that are vehemently 'anti-theory' or oppose the use of scientific principles, for example, those who believe that common-sense descriptions of 'what is going on', or of 'people doing things together' (Becker 1970), dissolve the need for a scientific approach. They believe that 'authentic knowledge is not furnished by scientific method but by immediate experience' ('the experience of the participant observer'; Rock 1979: 183). However, by so doing they limit 'authentic knowledge' to 'immediate experience', that is, to the subjective or inter-subjective realm. As a result, they are unable to incorporate or analyse relatively objective features of social life (like social settings and cultural and economic resources, and stable forms of power and domination). Most importantly, because of a strict commitment to the inter-subjective realm, they are unable to draw together objective and subjective social features and processes into a synthetic amalgam.

Finally, some qualitative and mixed-methods approaches, influenced as they are by laissez-faire pragmatism, deploy concepts and theory in a somewhat *ad hoc* manner, either as decorative additions or as a means of enhancing the status of research findings. But this cannot lead to genuinely integrated or cumulative knowledge. A concern for theory and its development via empirical research can only be founded on a systematic and reasoned basis, otherwise its validity claims will remain questionable.

Problem sampling and theory-influenced sampling

'Theoretical sampling' in GT (Glaser and Strauss 1967) is strictly limited to theory or concepts newly generated from research data. By contrast, problem sampling trusts in, and relies upon, a vast body of extant concepts, theory and knowledge to form part of a provisional explanatory scaffold, but is simultaneously alert to the potential for the emergence and creation of new concepts, explanations and analytical ideas. IR encourages the synergistic influences of these rather different types of theory and concepts in a more general search for cumulative knowledge.

Conceptual sampling

Patton identifies 'theory-based' sampling, in which 'the researcher samples incidents, slices of life, time periods or people on the basis of their ... representation of important theoretical constructs' (Patton 2001: 177). This refers to the direct use of theory or concepts as criteria for the selection of sampling units. In IR, 'conceptual sampling' is much closer to Patton's vision of theory-based sampling, although again there are significant differences. First, conceptual sampling can be regarded as an offshoot of, and supplement to, problem sampling. Problem sampling is concerned with the selection of data relevant to rather broad areas of social life (social domains), whereas conceptual sampling focuses on delimited, detailed aspects of social life *within* domains.

Second, Patton does not distinguish between concept types referring to ontological features of social life. For example, 'action' or 'behavioural concepts' may be identified by the participants themselves, such as types of inmate in a women's prison as 'snitchers', 'squares', 'jive bitches', and so on (Giallombardo 1966). They may also be researcher-defined, as in, for example, Spenser and Pahl's (2006) distinction between 'simple friendship' (including 'associates' and 'fun friends') and 'complex friendship' (including 'helpmates' and 'soul mates'). Concepts like 'affectionate regard' (Miller 1995) or 'episodic' or 'semi-detached' intimacy (Layder 2009) indicate the social-psychological quality of relationships and the feelings and forms of attachment or commitment they inspire.

By contrast, concepts such as 'formal organization' or 'bureaucracy' convey the essence of 'system concepts' and are crucial to understanding hospitals, business enterprises, criminal justice systems, universities, fast food chains like McDonald's (Ritzer 2011). Other concepts, like 'labour market segments', help to throw light on the links between the economy, polity, work and jobs. System concepts complement behavioural concepts in the sense that they intertwine with each other in social life and offer researchers a way of grasping the interconnections between human agency (social behaviour) and social systemic or (structural) phenomena – the so-called agency–structure problem. By sampling data or evidence around such concepts, the researcher is able to tap into these more 'elusive' or 'hidden' features of social reality.

A third type, 'bridging' concepts, depict the connection between subjective (behavioural) and objective (systemic) realms of the social world. Concepts such as 'career' (Stebbins 1970), 'emotional labour' (Hochschild 1983) or 'surveillance' (Foucault 1970) exemplify this interplay. Other bridging concepts are Etzioni's (1961) 'alienative', 'calculative' and 'moral' forms of involvement, motivation and attachment to the workplace, as is Ritzer's (2011) analysis of 'alienation' among McDonald's employees. By sampling in terms of behavioural, systemic or bridging concepts, a researcher can more precisely target relevant data and throw light on agency–structure or macro–micro linkages.

A MULTI-STRATEGY, MULTI-METHOD APPROACH

IR simultaneously integrates exploratory and explanatory objectives, including both theory-testing and theory-generation. Although some authors suggest that exploratory and explanatory objectives should be treated separately (Creswell et al. 2008: 68), with IR the researcher assumes that, if carefully handled, exploratory elements will constructively feed into the explanatory capacity of research. Furthermore, an explanatory aspiration will also help to define the problem-focus more clearly and robustly. Similarly, theory-testing and theory-generating elements can positively reinforce one another in generic 'theory-development'.

In pursuit of these objectives, as many data sources as possible are used to maximize the extent and density of data coverage. At the same time, data are analysed and cross-checked from as many vantage points as possible, so endorsing Denzin's (1989) ideas about triangulation (data, investigator, theoretical and methodological). However, IR includes an additional dimension of cross-checking – from a social domains perspective in which clusters of entangled social domains will be relevant to different projects under varying circumstances. Thus, along with conventional forms of triangulation, the domains perspective contributes to overall validity checks on reliability, veracity and credibility of data and data analysis.

PHASES OF RESEARCH: AN INTEGRATIVE FRAMEWORK

Wherever feasible and appropriate IR blends and integrates quantitative and qualitative data and method. Bryman (2008) has pointed out that in many cases the use of mixed methods does not achieve genuine blending or integration. The structured flexibility of IR designs makes them uniquely suited to 'blending' because they require the integration of different slices of data (social reality) from different domains. Unlike 'mixed-methods' approaches, IR is problem-led, not methods-led, where 'problems' are defined in terms of entangled domains.

Tashakkori and Teddlie (2008) have argued persuasively for an 'integrative framework' to judge the 'quality of inferences' (usually referred to as 'validity' or 'veracity' of conclusions) in mixed-methods research. They compare established criteria in quantitative and qualitative research and produce an integrative framework based on them. From the point of view of IR, such a framework must be based on a more comprehensive set of criteria – and have the effect of integrating *all aspects and phases* of research, including especially ontological and epistemological assumptions, and issues of causality and explanation.

In relation to this, Tashakkori and Teddlie also want to replace the term 'validity' with the notion of 'quality of inferences' for two principal reasons. First, they suggest that the term 'validity' has been hijacked by quantitative researchers who do not differentiate between the quality of data and the quality of conclusions. This may indeed point to an important limitation, although in itself it is not enough to justify abandoning the term, not least because validity is not the exclusive property of quantitative researchers. The generic meaning of validity applies to research quality as a whole. As such, its applicability cannot be limited to discrete phases or segments of research (for example, to prior assumptions, data collection, methods or conclusions). Validity must apply *simultaneously* to all components of the 'explanatory spine'.

For Tashakkori and Teddlie, the second reason to abandon the term 'validity' is that it has become mired in confusion resulting from the plethora of definitions that have arisen. They list 35 different types of validity in the research literature, and suggest that the level of confusion so created forces them 'to conclude that the term has lost its meaning or become obsolete' (Tashakkori and Teddlie 2008: 105). To abandon validity as a term simply because numerous 'technical' definitions have emerged is not persuasive. Validity remains credible and useful if we keep to its straightforward, dictionary definition as referring to arguments or reasons that are 'sound, defensible and well-grounded', and refuse to go along with 'extra' and unnecessary, technical definitions.

COMPLEMENTARY ASPECTS OF REALITY

Advocates of 'mixed methods' (Creswell et al. 2008; Tashakkori and Teddlie 2008) have suggested a number of reasons for such mixing of methods, including completeness, corroboration, complementarity and diversity in research. As a 'multi-strategy' approach, IR also emphasizes complementarity as the most important reason for integration. But in this sense 'integration' includes the bringing together of different but complementary features of social reality in order to define an empirical problem and a research-focus. Thus, complementarity is not solely about mixing quantitative and qualitative methods (as Tashakkorri and Teddlie define it), but is, rather, a way of accessing and reflecting the intrinsic nature of social reality. In this sense, complementarity is revealed in, and by, the inherent nature of social life and social reality.

As a result, mixing quantitative and qualitative methods should serve as *an instrument* of research necessity and explanatory objectives. An a priori need to mix methods itself should not be the pivotal definer of the overall research agenda. Complementarity, in this sense, allows the researcher to view triangulation as a means of achieving completeness of empirical 'coverage' (of the relevant domain entanglements), rather than technical/methodological completeness. The need for mixed methods to 'compensate' for weaknesses of any one method is replaced by the need to achieve as complete a coverage of social reality as possible. Recognizing the nature of social reality loads validity concerns into the research process at the beginning. Thus, triangulation, corroboration, concept-data fit, explanatory robustness, and so on, are continuous features of research, rather than limited to discrete pockets (stages or phases). Certainly, we must distinguish between the quality of data and the quality of inferences (validity of conclusions and interpretations). However, this must be extended to include initial problem questions and the ontological assumptions that frame them. Validity criteria must not be restricted to those defined in terms of quantitative and qualitative methods.

BLENDING LIFE-WORLD AND SYSTEM PHENOMENA

Generally, qualitative data best represent or depict various forms of life-world phenomena, including subjective experiences, such as feelings, emotions, self-esteem, empathy, and so on, and social involvements, such as interpersonal encounters, interaction or intimacy. Quantitative data may usefully supplement qualitative data, for example, to indicate the regularity of behaviours or their numerical spread within groups or networks. However, quantitative indices cannot replace the richness of understanding conveyed by qualitative data, such as the inner texture of feelings or social experiences. Qualitative data are an irreducible necessity for describing and explaining the subtle complexity of social behaviour. Adequate 'subjective understanding' is only possible if the psychological complexity of human beings is recognized. Artificial methodological assumptions of 'minimum psychology', as used in survey research (Goldthorpe 2000) in order to preserve the (mathematical) precision of the findings, must be avoided at all costs!

Of course, 'system phenomena', such as social settings and contextual resources, hugely influence human behaviour by both enabling and constraining it through forms of domination, language, values, norms, and even 'vocabularies of motive' (Mills 1940). However, in themselves, system phenomena do not 'do', act, think or feel, and thus accounts of system phenomena do not require a qualitative grasp of subjectivity or inter-subjective experience (although in an analytical sense qualitative descriptions and explanations of social organization, social relations and mechanisms remain relevant). System phenomena have an obdurate, 'reproduced' character formed through regularized social usage over time. While they rely on the generalized and routinized social practices of human beings, they are *relatively independent* of specific individuals, groups or practices. Reproduced relations, positions, roles, powers, practices and legitimating discourses are patterned into systems which are activated and actualized by successions of people over more or less extended periods of time. Their partly independent character means they are particularly suited to quantitative measurement since it is less likely to contradict or deny their essential nature. Both life-world phenomena (the domains of psychobiography and situated activity) and system phenomena (the domains of social settings and contextual resources) are deeply intertwined in real-life situations. As such, it remains essential for researchers to be able to identify life-world and system (agency–structure, macro–micro) interconnections as they are revealed in research data.

RESEARCH DESIGN AND DATA TYPES

Several research designs are particularly suitable for IR. First, there are those research designs in which quantitative and qualitative data analysis takes place 'concurrently', while the researcher's awareness constantly shuttles between different types of data and their analytical implications. In 'concurrent' designs, both types of data illuminate complementary aspects of social reality – interlocking domains – which re-enforces integration and blending. However, it is not always possible to juggle both types of data and analysis simultaneously. Thus, a 'sequential' design might be more appropriate, in which quantitative and qualitative data collection and analysis occur at different points in time. The most useful sequence for IR is the following:

Qualitative ——— Quantitative ——— Qualitative

In this sequence, qualitative inquiry provides the exploratory basis on which subsequent quantitative material (say in the form of a survey or structured interviews) might serve as a confirmatory check on the initial findings, and which are further supplemented and expanded by qualitative data. Integration and blending are maximized if the sequential design is subsequently reconfigured, as far as possible into a concurrent design. Generating original quantitative data from surveys with large samples is not always practically feasible, or even necessary. (Experiments, with their strict control over variables are generally not appropriate for IR since they negate or subvert the 'open' conditions of real-life situations.)

Secondary quantitative data (originally generated for different purposes) are useful since they are frequently based on large data samples. 'Free-standing' secondary data, produced by market research organizations such as Mintel, CIPIS and Markit, are important sources of statistics and factual information on industries such as food, leisure and finance. Other sources are government or 'official' statistics on crime, criminal justice, transport, families, housing, lifestyles, and so on. Also, data sets of professional (academic) researchers are housed in such places as the UK Data Archive or the Australian Social Science Data Archive, or published in professional journals. All three sources offer rich funds of data on wider organizational features and processes (social settings and contextual resources) and may complement qualitative data on individual behaviour and social interaction (psychobiography and situated activities), reflecting the many ways in which life-world and system features combine in social life.

The 'open' nature of social processes ensures that human social behaviour cannot be accurately measured or controlled (except by artificially freezing such processes by experimentally controlled means, or by introducing arbitrary methodological 'rules' such as the 'minimum psychology' assumption of large scale surveys (Goldthorpe 2000)). Thus, *on their own*, quantitative measures or indices of behaviour can be decidedly limited. For IR, a core of qualitative data should be regarded as its 'centre', while quantitative data – either secondary or original, survey data – form a 'containing envelope'. That is, a core of primarily qualitative data (depicting psychobiography and situated activity) form the 'contents' of the envelope, or package, while quantitative data (referring more to settings and contextual resources) provide the outer packaging.

DATA ANALYSIS AS NASCENT EXPLANATION

Data analysis in IR is about producing (at least) a provisional explanation, and signals the completion of the first cycle of IR. Interpreting and understanding data place the initial orienting scaffold under empirical scrutiny, and raises such questions as: What aspects of the scaffold remain intact in the light of the evidence so far collected? Does the data demand a remodelling of the conceptual framework? How is this best achieved? The inherent plasticity of IR means that this is not the 'end' of the process, or even a discrete phase. All phases are 'in-play' at all times and data analysis is no exception. Conceptual and explanatory advances are not sharply defined or discrete processes, and research is always a 'work in progress', often resulting from imperfect, *in situ* judgements, and no little luck. The first round or phase of analysis (and each subsequent one) must be regarded as a way-station punctuating the gradual emergence of an explanation from its most 'primitive' to its most sophisticated form. The nascent explanation is progressively brought to maturity by the constant remodelling of the orienting scaffold.

An example: prison research

Knight's (2012, 2016) study of in-cell television in a male prison in the UK displays many of these elements. Using data from semi-structured interviews with prisoners and staff, as well as prisoners' structured diaries (of television use), Knight examined the influence of TV and its multiple roles and functions in the prison setting. She approached data collection with a fund of general theoretical perspectives as background or 'orienting' concepts. These included not only domain theory (and adaptive analysis), but also concepts and ideas on TV use (Lull 1990), media theory (Moores 1993), maximum security prisoners (Sykes 1999), and more general concepts such as 'self-regulation' (Rose 1991) and emotions and interpersonal control (Layder 2004).

Knight began data analysis by breaking the data down and segmenting the data in terms of themes and concepts and relevant codes and sub-codes. These codes included (a) 'talking about television' (with sub-codes such as 'in-cell activity', 'situated activity', 'time-filling and shifting', 'power and control'), (b) 'looking after yourself' (with sub-codes like 'coping', 'future plans', 'well-being and therapy'), and (c) 'prison life: tensions and dilemmas' (including sub-codes of 'violence and aggression', 'stress', 'trust and friendship', 'isolation', 'withdrawal'). The dialogue between data collection, extant theory and emerging codes and concepts began to accelerate and intensify and, as a consequence, two further sets of themes, codes and categories were added. These were (d) 'staff' (reflecting the sub-codes of 'policy and prison work', 'behaviour management'), and (e) 'emotion', which grew out of the category 'looking after yourself' and the realization that prisoners' relationship with TV viewing was a 'good way of controlling emotionality'.

Many of the themes, categories, labels and concepts that provided the codes for analysing data were an interesting mix of both descriptive and conceptual elements. For example, many of the emotion labels and codes were descriptive, such as 'anger', 'fear', 'sadness', 'boredom', while there was a heavily conceptual one, Hochschild's (1983) 'emotional labour'. Other conceptual elements derived from Lull's (1990) typology of the social uses of TV, which was tailored to the prison situation to include 'affiliation and avoidance', 'conflict reduction', 'solidarity'. Concepts taken from Sykes' (1999) 'pains of incarceration' were also suitably adapted.

The cross-fertilization of ideas stemming from ongoing data analysis stimulated the emergence of core themes, labels, codes and concepts. For Knight, the 'most significant concept' – of 'control' – emerged in this manner. Original core concepts, such as 'emotion' and 'talking about TV', were used to inform the final concept of control and were reinforced by existing work on emotion and interpersonal control (Layder 2004) and Rose's (1991) work on 'self-regulation'. Knight began to develop a conceptual map, influenced by the notion of conceptual elaboration (Layder 1998). She describes a process by which

> fragments of data stored under 'emotion' were re-enlisted and aligned to the concept of 'interpersonal control' ... these fragments had relationships or linkages to other concepts such as 'looking after yourself' and 'prison life: tensions and dilemmas'. (Knight 2012: 143)

By allowing concepts to evolve in this manner from a blend of emergent data and extant theory (particularly the intersection of psychobiography, situated activity and prison as a social setting), Knight has been able to advance a number of ideas around the interrelated themes of incarceration, TV, emotion and the achievement of personal control (Knight 2012).

Developing theory, concepts and explanation

With IR, a fully-fledged explanation develops from the confrontation between extant concepts, ideas, themes and sampling codes as they meet with raw research data at the 'coal face' of data collection. While engaged in data analysis, the researcher must be alive to the possibilities of conceptual modification, assimilation, transformation, and so on. This feeds into conceptual/theoretical elaboration in which data analysis draws attention to interconnections between orienting concepts and other, related concepts. The clusters so created begin to influence data analysis, and eventually give rise to embryonic explanations of the focal behaviour. In this sense, 'explanations' are clusters of concepts, linked by arguments and chains of reasoning and supported by empirical data.

Individual concepts may have their own 'histories of development' within a project, since they may evolve via data analysis, somewhat independently of the cluster as a whole. However, the more data collection and analysis progresses, the more likely it is that individual concepts develop in tandem with the collective development of the whole cluster. However, it is important for researchers to be aware of both individual and collective development of concepts in order to be clear about their respective influences in the overall project.

Individual concepts 1: Splitting or fragmenting. As an investigative and exploratory form of research, IR encourages the emergence or discovery of novel perspectives, concepts and theory. However, where established concepts are strongly supported by data, such a 'conclusion' should be regarded as a secure base-camp from which to go on to explore new analytical angles on the behaviour under study. Also, by identifying gaps in information, it indicates the need for further data sampling. The exploratory character of IR ensures a greater concern with stretching the limits of extant concepts, and exploring new explanatory possibilities. The emphasis is on the ways in which particular (orienting) concepts might be elaborated, extended or otherwise modified in the light of ongoing data analysis. Consequently, organically related concepts may emerge with new emphases, nuances or inflections, or with extended or more focused ranges of applicability. Concepts produced in this manner could be said to have split-off or fragmented from orienting concepts while also taking on new meanings.

Individual concepts 2: Substitution. 'Stretching the limits' of established concepts might not yield any positive results. If a concept cannot be rescued or accommodated by appropriate remoulding, revision or modification, then it must be replaced. A more appropriate concept would then undergo a similar process of matching against ongoing data, and consequent modification and reshaping, in order to achieve a greater consonance with data.

Individual concepts 3: Innovation. The final type involves the emergence of concepts 'freshly created' by the researcher as a response to the analytical and empirical problems posed by the data. Concepts, no matter how innovative they are, or appear to be, also retain important links with prior concepts, words and ideas, which also contribute to their meanings. Much like a dictionary pins down the meaning of words by using other words, concepts can only be 'understood' and have meaning in relation to other concepts which define them. It is all too often forgotten that a pre-existing connective tissue of concepts and ideas greatly influences the meanings that can be attached to new concepts. New or emergent concepts do not simply and solely emerge from raw data – certain conditions have to be met.

- There must be an existing 'data-fit deficit problem', wherein no extant concepts provide an adequate 'fit' for new research data. For example, Miller (1995) devised the concept of 'intimate terrorism' to explain interview data with married couples that could not be handled appropriately by concepts such as 'marital love', 'companionate love' or 'romantic love'.
- There must be a dialogical interplay between a pre-existing web of related concepts (in the case of 'intimate terrorism', these would be 'romantic love', 'pure relationships', 'companionate love'). There must also be a practical engagement with data collection (interviews with married couples) and analysis, as well as sifting through facts, information, data or evidence.

Theoretical elaboration

A central objective of IR is to gradually build up an interconnected web of concepts that will provide the basis for a robust explanation of the behaviour under scrutiny. There are three sorts of processes that contribute to elaboration:

1. First, it involves breaking down core concepts to reveal their internal dimensions, properties and characteristics. For example, the concept of 'career' (related to psychobiography) can be broken down into 'types of career' (for example, work, marriage or illness) or 'structural types' (bureaucratic, collegiate or market), 'control over career (status) movements' (in illness, occupations or

intimate relationships). By identifying subsidiary concepts in relation to other core concepts, a network or web of interrelated concepts may be developed (see Layder 1998: 117–121).

2. Secondary elaboration can be achieved by using one or more satellite concepts generated from the core as the basis for further groups or clusters adjacent to the original cluster.
3. Elaboration by expanding the clusters both internally and externally can be achieved by *typology building*. That is, by constructing models of social types arranged along a continuum, the researcher is 'forced' to ask comparative questions concerning how and why groups, social settings, relationships, types of actor or participant are the same or different from others in the continuum.

Typology building imparts order to observations and encourages researchers to think in terms of arguments and chains of reasoning, rather than one-to-one correspondences between concepts and data. As with conceptual sampling, typologies can be distinguished by whether they are 'behavioural', 'systemic' or 'bridging', and this draws into the equation further theoretical issues (for example, links between agency–structure, macro–micro aspects or 'levels'). Such exercises make data analysis denser, reflecting a complex, multidimensional social reality.

Elaboration via general theories

Where relevant, and where it would positively add to understanding and analysis, 'emergent' theory may be elaborated by drawing *selectively* upon one or two concepts from general theories (of, for example, Bourdieu, Habermas, Giddens, and so on) to stimulate theoretical/conceptual creativity and to strengthen the emergent explanation. Selectivity here implies restricting the number of concepts 'imported' (from general theories) in order to generate new theory or modify extant theory, and using them sparingly in data analysis. General theory should not be imported *in toto* as a means of organizing the entire research process in a prior and deterministic manner, for this can only serve to reaffirm what is already known. It doesn't really test, advance or develop theory. 'Selectivity' is also necessary in the sense that concepts must be chosen only from those general theories that meet the following criteria:

- They must be firmly committed to scientific method, and to empirical research as an important component of theory-generation as well as an adjudicator of validity.
- They must not be based exclusively on abstract narratives, metaphors or 'internal logic' to validate their propositions. Instead, they must be corroborated by systematic empirical research.

- General theories must be open to the possibility of conceptual interchange with theory generated from empirical data. Some are impermeable in this sense, preventing co-optation of concepts for fear of 'contamination'. General theories like this are often deployed in a blanket and deterministic manner, ruling out the possibility of conceptual innovation.
- General theories are essential to the cumulative nature of social scientific knowledge. Of course, all knowledge is cumulative in the trivial sense that the overall store of information always increases. But genuine accumulation only occurs where such knowledge is integrated and there is an interchange between different, and sometimes 'isolated', islands of knowledge.

Selective interchanges with general theory can be made at broadly three junctures in the research process: before the research has begun, during the research, and after it has 'formally' finished.

> *Before research*: A researcher might import concepts from a general theory to initiate the theorizing process, in much the same manner as other orienting concepts. However, they should not be used simply as a means of self-verification or self-confirmation of the theory from which they are drawn. They should be used as a route into further theoretical elaboration.
>
> *During research*: General theory might be introduced during data collection and analysis to revive a flagging theoretical impetus or to stimulate new ideas and often has a creative effect. Again, the emphasis must be on extension or revision.
>
> *After research*: Concepts from general theory may be introduced retrospectively, after the project has been formally concluded, to enhance, tweak or develop the final form of the explanation, but not simply to 'decorate' research findings.

CONSTANT REFORMULATION: A CONCLUDING COMMENT

Iterative cycles require constant reformulations of the orienting scaffold to serve as the basis for subsequent versions of the emergent explanation. Each reformulation indicates the need for adjustments or additions to the sampling frame, data collection and overall research strategy which, in turn, feed into the next cycle and version of the orienting scaffold. These changes have knock-on effects for the problem-focus and core research questions in that they will require confirmation, subtle adjustment or radical alteration.

'Elaboration' represents a more advanced and complex form of concept- or theory-development, dealing as it does with interrelations between ensembles of concepts.

As such, it is likely to require more reiterations of phases and cycles than do single-concept explanations. But the increase in complexity does not require wholesale repetitions of complete cycles. Many phases can be compressed or elided, or components may be left out, depending on local (research) circumstances. This is particularly the case where greater reflection on the internal logic and reasoning of clusters is required, rather than further sampling and data collection.

The IR sequence represents a continuous running commentary on the *in situ* 'state of play' of validity claims. In this respect, elaboration signals the terminus of this process, just as initial problem-formulation (and the orienting scaffold) represents the front-loading of ontological and epistemological assumptions. Elaboration is the logical, theoretical and substantive endpoint of the overall trajectory of IR – its entire research arc.

6

THEORY IN INVESTIGATIVE RESEARCH

CHAPTER CONTENTS

Many approaches to social research regard theory as an add-on extra, or purely optional choice. By contrast, IR centralizes the importance of theory as being crucial for research design and data collection, as well as adding to the robustness of its findings and explanatory conclusions. Without theory, the aspirations of empirical research and its potential explanatory yield are limited. However, theory construction must proceed strictly in accordance with empirical evidence as a scientific guarantee of its validity claims. In other words, 'theory' in the form of 'abstract story-telling' undermines evidence-based explanations because truly explanatory concepts and theory can only properly develop as an outcome or as an input of empirical research.

This chapter divides into two distinct but related emphases. First, I show how IR utilizes five types of theory in empirical research: 'variable' (or hypothesis-testing) theory, 'applied' general theory, empirical theory, single or multiple 'orienting' concepts and, finally, emergent or 'generated' theory. I discuss how each of these types may be amended and refined to accord with the purposes of IR. The second part of the chapter concentrates on how empirical research may facilitate the construction, development or generation of theory and concepts.

VARIABLE THEORY AND THEORY-TESTING

'Variable theories' describe purportedly 'causal' relationships between two or more empirically identifiable variables, such as class, ethnicity, gender, educational attainment. 'Variable' theories are also referred to as 'hypothetico-deductive' or middle-range' (Merton 1968). They differ from 'grand' or 'general' theories because of their closer anchoring to the empirical world as a source of validation. They are also clearly distinguishable from purely inductive approaches by relying on the deductive assumptions of a prior theoretical framework to shape and interpret data. However, crucially, variable theory is concerned with 'testability', which is made possible by the use of precise and 'objectively' measurable variables. In this sense, 'testability' is concerned with assessing the extent to which relationships between variables are supported by empirical evidence or data. Essential to the guarantee of such testability is the application of quantitative methods (primarily surveys) and the statistical analysis of (quantitative) data.

For the purposes of IR, an amended version would have a wider application but would also require radical alteration. First, alternative criteria of *testability*, validity and explanation are required to expand its range and explanatory power. Second, the flat, one-dimensional notion of social reality which undergirds the original versions must be abandoned and replaced by multidimensional models stretching though time and space. Third, social 'variables' should not be limited to factors that are impersonal, inert and mathematically precise. They must include empirical indicators of interpersonal phenomena and inter-subjective meanings. As a result, qualitative methods, data and analysis must play an equivalent and complementary role. This amended version also needs to attend to theory-generation, as well as theory-testing, with a consequent de-emphasis on confirming or disconfirming relationships between variables. The focus should be on the way incoming data inform alterations, reconstructions of the framework or the data's role in searching for emergent theory. In this sense, an interesting hypothesis should be regarded as a flexible – rather than a fixed – route to potentially very different ideas about how data may be interpreted. Such modifications would serve two rather distinct research strategies.

Using a variable hypothesis as a research guide

The first strategy entails beginning a research project with a 'variable' hypothesis (for example, 'educational attainment' varies in relation to 'gender'), but which does not monopolize the focus of research interest. Instead, the 'hypothesis' is deployed as a flexible research template which offers a structured focus while allowing room for shifts in direction and the exploration of new possibilities in data collection and analysis. Here, the idea of 'testing' indicates the 'usefulness' (or otherwise) of the hypothesis for theory-generation rather than pointing to a precise relationship between specific variables in particular circumstances. At all times, the hypothesis is regarded as potentially revisable, or alterable, *in situ*, that is, in the light of evidence freshly unearthed. Variables should include a wider variety of social phenomena than quantitative indices of happiness, consumption, educational attainment, social mobility. They should include phenomena that are responsible for producing such variables and indices, such as modes of social or interpersonal control, types of relationship or types of organization, 'situated activity', 'social settings', or aspects of 'ontological security', and so on. Over time, the importance of the initial hypothesis may gradually wane and take its place as but one among several tools and resources, but continue to play a background, supportive role.

Exploratory research and variable hypotheses

The second strategy involves a more *exploratory* remit. This may be because the area or problem is relatively un-researched, or it might be deliberately used to stimulate creativity. During the course of data collection and/or analysis, a rudimentary 'variable hypothesis' emerges which is then co-opted as part of the research with the longer-term aim of producing more explanatory insights and ideas. The primary emphasis during the project should not be on 'firming-up' the emergent hypothesis, but on using it as a template against which incoming evidence/data may be evaluated.

Elements of testing the emergent hypothesis, will be necessary, but should not displace the importance of exploring new theoretical ideas and concepts. The nascent hypothesis should be used in conjunction with sampling and data collection strategies, as well as analytical exploration (concept formation and clustering) to maximize theory-generation potential. Of course, if the emergent variable hypothesis remains strongly supported by the data/evidence, then this can be treated as a valid research outcome – in the form of a suggestion about further exposure to more specific testing – as in the spirit of the traditional version.

APPLIED GENERAL THEORY

Using general theory in empirical research

General theories are largely abstract and concerned either with large-scale processes of social development or with very general aspects of social processes/reality, such as the relationship between life-world and system aspects of analysis. Examples of general theory can be found in the work of classical thinkers such as Comte, Marx, Durkheim, Weber and Simmel, or modern thinkers like Elias, Foucault, Bourdieu, Goffman, Giddens, Habermas, and so on. All too often such theories are used purely analytically – without reference to research methods or their application to substantive empirical problems or research. Much more effort should be made to harness the potential of general theory in guiding and influencing empirical research as well as for empirical research to inform and influence general theory. Thus, we should attempt to narrow the gap between discussions about (abstract) general theoretical matters (concepts and explanations) on the one hand, and, on the other, practical decisions about research methods and strategy (data collection and analysis). This would enable potential convergences to be explored and identified.

Standing in the way of this are the embedded ideas of two dominant research traditions. Both Merton's (hypothetico-deductive) theory-testing research and Glaser and Strauss's grounded theory insist that general theory should play no role in empirical research because it is too abstract and removed from real-world issues and the practicalities of research. Such armchair speculation results in the researcher 'forcing' data into alien concepts and categories, thus creating a lack of fit between data and concepts and fracturing the concept–indicator link. These views betray a misunderstanding of the relation between general theories and the empirical world. The claim that they are not 'anchored' or 'grounded' in empirical reality cannot be sustained because if they did not refer to empirical reality *in any sense at all*, then they would be literally meaningless and incomprehensible. It is precisely because they often do make recognizable claims about social reality and social processes that many general theories can be said to possess a definite relation to empirical reality.

It is certainly true that some general theories are not as closely anchored to the empirical world. However, this should not deflect from the capacity of others to depict the (empirical) world in ways that may be more or less useful and truthful (cognitively accurate and/or adequate). It is better to conceive of general theories as ranging along a continuum of 'closeness' to empirical reality, some being very abstract and more distantly related to empirical data, and others being more closely connected, and thus more readily acceptable, to empirical researchers as appropriate for research designs. Some of the work of general theorists can be regarded as a source of (provisional) orienting concepts for explaining and analysing data in empirical research. This involves a number of closely related issues. First is the use of whole networks or clusters of concepts – as opposed to individual concepts taken from them. This refers to the problem of using general theories as all-encompassing 'master frameworks' for the interpretation of data/evidence. Second is the issue of whether general theories can be regarded, for these purposes, as 'open' or 'closed' discourses. The third concerns the advantages and dangers of separating individual concepts from their 'home' theory/network. This is linked with issues surrounding the difference between 'sensitizing' and 'orienting' concepts.

General theories as master frameworks

In selecting a general theory prior to research, as a total system, network or cluster of concepts with which to guide data collection and analysis, researchers are often tempted to employ it as an all-embracing 'master framework' for the interpretation and analysis (and ultimately an explanation) of empirical data. As a consequence, the research automatically slips into a 'verification' mode, in which research data simply functions to confirm or support the overall theory, thus reducing possibilities of theoretical advance or innovation.

General theories as open or closed discourses

'Master frameworks' restrict innovation by employing general theories as *closed networks of ideas* or hermetically sealed systems of ideas resistant to addition, alteration and revision (which is often the case with the use of ideas, for example, from Marx, Elias or Bourdieu). In contrast, IR emphasizes viewing general theoretical discourses as potentially *open* and revisable in order to widen research resources, encourage innovation and boost explanatory power. Concepts may be borrowed from, and used independently of, the home theory and applied to unfamiliar areas and varying research contexts. As such, individual concepts (or clusters of them) may be challenged and subject to revision or refashioning as the research unfolds.

Regarding and using general theories as 'open' discourses may enhance the quality and explanatory power of social research, but what determines whether they are, or can be, regarded as open rather than closed? There are two closely related factors of relevance here. The first has to do with the intrinsic nature of the theory itself, specifically the 'permeability' of its cognitive content. Some general theories more readily permit the assimilation of concepts from other discourses, allowing their concepts to be used in different contexts. Their internal nature 'allows' this to happen with minimum damage to, or disfigurement of, the meaning and integrity of the original theory, including its truth and/or cognitive content. With the closed type, it is more difficult to detach concepts from others in the home theory without diminishing their meaningful relation to the total network.

Crucially the extent of permeability (openness, flexibility) goes hand in hand with the second factor, which is the attitudes, beliefs and behaviour of 'users', adherents or followers (sometimes more accurately described as 'proselytizers') with regard to the theory in relation to other theories. With the 'closed' type, adherents, 'believers' or followers tend to treat their favoured theory in a sacrosanct manner, as if it were an exclusive truth which is in (explanatory) competition with other theories. They tend to regard permeability and flexibility of application as a 'weakness' or the 'slippery slope' to dissolution or emasculation of the theory. Some Marxists and Eliasians are prone to both these tendencies. We must ask questions such as: To what extent are they protective of the theory? How vigorously do they 'defend' it against all criticism? Do they regard it as a unitary paradigm which must be defended in its own right? Does it (the theory/framework) function as an emblem or badge of membership, and an 'us' versus 'them' (believers and non-believers) mentality for adherents (Marxists, Foucauldians, Eliasians, etc.)?

Of course, in order to be 'open' a discourse must contain some useful cognitive content, and at least some of its truth claims (both analytical and empirical) must be adequate and valid. However, a general theoretical/conceptual framework should not be thought of as monopolizing the 'objective' or 'exclusive' truth (the final word). A truly 'open' conceptual framework may hold important insights into the nature of social reality, but should remain inherently plastic and capable of accommodating new insights, ideas and concepts and their supporting empirical facts or evidence.

An example of an open discourse

'Domain theory' forms the backdrop to particular empirical research projects, while also helping to shape their foci. As such, it does not preclude input from other theories, methodological strategies, and so on, if they are appropriate, relevant, merited or 'demand' inclusion. For example, Victoria Knight's (2016) work on prisoners' use of in-cell television draws on media theory, and Rose (1991) on governmentality, while Thilo Boeck's (2011) work on social capital demonstrates how it can be used in conjunction with Putnam, Bourdieu and mixed-method approaches. Neither does the domains framework 'determine' the meaning of empirical data found within its parameters. It is an inclusive framework that allows dialogue and synergy between diverse theories and empirical data/evidence. It encourages a flow of communication between (sometimes opposed) positions, even those restricted by, or committed to, 'exclusive' positions, for example, those who believe in reductive, one-dimensional models of reality.

EMPIRICAL THEORY: SUBSTANTIVE AND FORMAL

Research in particular areas often produces substantively specific concepts and theoretical ideas, such as 'labour market segmentation', 'organizational or occupational behaviour', 'client–professional relationships', and so on. Such theory is usually at a lower level of abstraction than general theory. Its empirical connectedness is more pronounced in the way that it depicts the operation of particular features of society. It is not a general attempt to depict the nature of social behaviour, or societal dynamics, or the links between agency and structure or between macro and micro features and levels of analysis. It is possible to distinguish between more formal aspects of such empirical theories. This is reflected in, for example, a formal theory of labour market segmentation across a wide range of industrial or occupational groupings, as compared to an explanation of segmentation within a specific occupation (such as the acting profession; Layder 1985, 1993). The scope of the latter is restricted to one area whereas the more formal (and abstract) theory is pertinent to a wider range or class of phenomena.

Some empirical concepts and theory are seemingly tied to their originating areas or problems, as is, for example, Hochschild's (1983) concept of 'emotional labour', which is tied to work/occupations/labour. But connections with wider sets of concepts and bodies of theory, such as 'emotion work' and 'feeling rules', must not be discounted. So there isn't a completely clean distinction between empirical theory and other more general concepts. Yet other concepts are subtle combinations of general theory and substantive application. For example, Rose's (1991) 'governing the soul' is clearly influenced by Foucault's ideas on self-governance and surveillance but it has been applied to the specific problem of how prisoners deal with the psychological problems of incarceration (Knight 2016). Also, although the empirical world or particular substantive areas may 'unearth' particular concepts, very often they exist *within* groups, networks, clusters or webs of concepts. This is a 'core and satellite' pattern (Layder 1998) where the core concept is surrounded by auxiliary concepts of varying importance for data analysis.

ORIENTING CONCEPTS (SINGLE OR MULTIPLE)

This section concentrates on the use of individual (or clusters of) concepts to analyse empirical research data. In this regard, I prefer the term 'orienting' concepts over the term 'sensitizing' concepts. The latter has had a fairly wide currency in social research ever since Blumer (1956) first introduced it in the context of a critique of 'definitive' concepts (and the 'positivism' of the time). He suggested that the notion of 'sensitizing concepts' was more 'flexible' and appropriate to the subject matter of sociology. Thus, sensitizing concepts are more equipped to capture human social meanings and the processes of interaction from which they emerge. On this view, sociology and social research are humanistic, interpretative disciplines which seek to understand acting subjects and the 'joining up' of their activities. They are not, as in the positivist vision, exclusively about explaining behaviour as the result of 'external' non-acting social structures and systems in an objective social world and operating according to generalized laws.

Range of application of orienting concepts

Certainly, Blumer's concern with flexibility is important since social research/analysis must attempt to grasp, at least in part, the inner nature of human action (inter-subjective meaning). However, in the context of a more embracing notion of social science, which acknowledges a complex, multidimensional reality of social domains, Blumer's vision of sensitizing concepts turns out to be curiously inflexible. That is, their use is restricted to behavioural (life-world) phenomena because Blumer's symbolic-interactionist framework denies the existence of more objective features of social life, such as reproduced settings or wider structures and/or systems. In this sense, 'orienting' concepts are more flexible, inclusive and adaptable, in that they can refer to non-acting (objective) social phenomena (systems, structures, cultural knowledge) *as well as* active, intentional and reflexive human agents. However, we have to be aware of the different (ontological and epistemological) statuses of those concepts.

Orienting concepts are used by the researcher to suggest patterns in, and explanations of, data. They suggest further lines of inquiry, even if they are dispensed with in the long run. Conversely, the more evidential support that an orienting concept receives as the project unfolds, the more involved it becomes in conceptual extension and theoretical elaboration. In contrast, sensitizing concepts have a 'one-off' quality to them; they either fit particular segments of data, and are thus confirmed, or they do not fit the data (and are thus rejected). They have a weaker connection to sustained theory-building over longer stretches of time, and in relation to a social reality that is variegated and multidimensional. With orienting concepts there is no question of 'forcing' data into alien conceptual categories. Using concepts to suggest – or even temporarily 'impose' – a pattern or interpretation on data does not irrevocably commit the researcher to particular concepts irrespective of empirical support. In this sense, orienting concepts are 'provisional' devices and their meaning, usefulness and efficacy are defined and arbitrated in substantial part through the ongoing collection of data (as well as through argument and the development of analytical and explanatory ideas).

Multiple concepts: exploration and explanation

With IR, researchers also work with networks (or webs) of related concepts which are either loosely or more tightly connected with each other. Although, of course, single concepts (especially if they are 'core', 'major' or 'dominant') are integral to explanation, conceptual networks or clusters play a central role in this kind of research. Explanations are constructed in the form of arguments expressed linguistically through concepts and their wider networks. The greater the number of concepts used, and the more densely packed they are within the analysis, the more pronounced will be the overall argument.

There are several patterns of multiple concepts that may be used to good effect. Perhaps the most prominent of these are:

1 Variations on the 'core-satellite' model – where one concept is core, while others provide peripheral support.
2 Pure 'network' or 'cluster' models – where all the concepts are of equal significance or influence for explanation.

EMERGENT CONCEPTS

It might seem that 'orienting' concepts are the complete opposite of concepts that 'emerge' during data collection in empirical research. But concepts do not, and cannot, emerge simply or immanently from data! Conceptual emergence can only be created out of the collision (and sometimes confrontation) between data extraction and conceptual assimilation via data analysis. The meaning, validity and (empirical) adequacy of newly minted concepts are co-determined. They are not only products of the data itself, but equally by virtue of their existing nexus of relationships with other concepts. Just as a word in a dictionary is defined by another set of words, so the meanings of concepts are defined in large part by their relation to other concepts. Thus, IR takes seriously the role of existing conceptual networks which embed so-called novel, newly created, or discovered concepts. In this respect, the search for them cannot begin with open-coding – or letting only the data themselves suggest relevant coding categories and concepts.

The process of conceptual emergence begins in much the same manner as with the use of orienting concepts. However, the crucial differences are marked by the way in which the research design and objectives evolve in tandem with the explanatory value of the concepts themselves, and how the concepts shape up to particular research outcomes. Sometimes orienting concepts are associated with research outcomes in which the original concept is retained in some form or the other – through modification, extension or elaboration. Emergent concepts, on the other hand, are linked with research outcomes in which the original orienting concepts diminish in significance as data collection and analysis proceeds, to the point where they are replaced by alternative concepts. There are three main ways in which this may happen. The following discussion expands on some ideas raised in the previous chapter.

Emergence via splitting or fragmenting

A new concept may *split or fragment* from an initial orienting concept. For example, a researcher investigating the dynamics of friendship or romantic intimacy may begin coding data around the concept of 'emotional labour'. But during data collection and analysis, he or she is forced to concede that while appropriate to work and occupations, there are problems with emotional labour as it applies to these types of intimacy. As a response, the researcher might come up with a number of alternatives which seem to offer more appropriate concepts, such as 'styles of emotional management', 'emotional distance' or 'emotional availability'. Data may increasingly emphasize the significance of these concepts while 'emotional labour' declines in significance. Because the newer concepts bear some relation to emotional labour, they can be said to have split off or fragmented from (and thus emerged out of) the original concept. At the same time, the newer concepts also break fresh ground, and take data analysis in another direction.

Emergence via replacement by an alternative

If empirical support for an orienting concept weakens considerably, a fundamental rethink is demanded and the core concepts on which the design and analytical framework are based must be reformulated. For example, it may be decided that a project provisionally guided by the core concept of emotional labour will be better analysed in terms of the concepts of power and control. That is, even though the concepts are already established and not 'new' concepts.

Developing innovative concepts

Even if the initial objective is to prioritize the search for newly emergent concepts, the researcher begins with a selectively chosen orienting concept to initially shape and channel data collection and coding. Only if incoming data cannot be assimilated by the original orienting concepts does the researcher make the decision to replace it with a freshly minted concept that solves the analytical problems posed by the data. But crucially, the data do not simply 'suggest' or 'offer up' a new, more appropriate concept. The concept is generated equally by a web of links with other concepts. Consider, for example, Miller's (1995) concept of 'emotional terrorism'. How was it created?

First, its emergence resulted from a data-fit problem caused by an incompatibility between the idealized imagery of the behaviour of married couples, reflected in concepts such as 'marital' or 'romantic love', and the actual (observed or reported) behaviour. Miller's interviews with married couples revealed the predominance of power struggles, co-dependence and 'unpeaceful coexistence'. The contradictions between these data and the idealized romanticism of existing concepts suggested an empirical space for the concept of 'intimate terrorism', which focuses on the more negative aspects of intimacy in day-to-day life.

However, the meaning of the concept is not immediately disclosed simply via data. Equally importantly, its meaning emerges from its relation with associated concepts. Emotional terrorism trades on an ironic juxtaposition of 'intimacy', implying harmonious coexistence, and 'terrorism', suggesting an opposing state of mutual antagonism, manipulation, perhaps even exploitation. The unique cognitive and affective force of the concept is produced by the drawing together of the two meanings. Emotional terrorism provides a corrective to over-idealized concepts such as romantic love (also implicit in the so-called 'pure relationship') (Giddens 1992; Beck and Beck-Gernsheim 1995). In addition, empirical data on couples (Miller 1995; Reibstein 1997; Marshall 2006) reveals evidence of variations in intimacy not captured by the term 'pure relationship'. This empirical gap (lack of fit between concept and reality) also creates space for concepts like 'episodic intimacy' (Layder 2009) or 'unpeaceful co-existence', rather than 'mutual satisfaction' (associated with the 'pure relationship'), as key ingredients of modern intimacy.

The space for concepts like 'episodic intimacy' arose not only because of connections with related concepts. Modern relationships do not conform to highly generalized concepts such as the 'pure relationship'. The 'episodic' part of the concept homes-in on the fact that modern couples are not continuously or 'evenly' committed or involved. The personalities and psychobiographies of the partners and variations in their interpersonal activities play huge roles in the forms of modern intimacy. Modern intimate relationships are fluid and labile, not uniform or 'pure' in any sense.

THE DEPLOYMENT OF THEORY IN OVERALL RESEARCH STRATEGY

When deploying theory or concepts in social research, researchers often feel compelled to choose an option from a series of either-or choices, such as:

theory-testing	or	theory-generating
extant theory	or	emergent theory
general theory	or	empirical or substantive theory
single (core) concepts	or	networks or clusters

Of course, there are advantages to be gained from selecting particular options, and this may indeed result in competent research. It certainly has the 'advantage' of creating consistency and relative simplicity of research design. However, the downside is that such a project would be somewhat strait-jacketed and fixed within a set path, minimizing the possibility of creativity in response to unexpected data (that is, not being analytically responsive to incoming data) and putting a brake on conceptual innovation. IR encourages a broader level of creativity by emphasizing the structured flexibility of strategy in which multiple strands are drawn together in a carefully orchestrated manner. The point is to weave together elements and strands from different resources and the 'dilemmas' and options referred to above. Ideally, an IR-inspired research project would meld these oppositions, for example, by including some theory-testing as well as some theory-generating, or integrating aspects of general theory with empirical theory. It might also be profitable to cut across and combine some oppositions or strands, such as mixing elements of general theory with theory-testing.

Simultaneously attending to different aspects produces a densely compacted conceptual analysis mimicking the complexity of the social reality under investigation. But this must always be combined with a closely integrated underlay of empirical data generated through multiple strategies. Selective focusing helps to avoid any over-complication of the analysis since it involves concentrating on two or three domains (and dimensions) at any one time. Keeping the analysis within set limits also has the effect of sharpening the problem-focus of the project. Equally, in pursuing optimal data collection, methods and strategies are honed by constant reference to the problem-focus. This generally results in a reasoned and manageable mix of strategies and methods.

DEVELOPING THEORY IN IR: AN OVERVIEW

In IR, the domains framework/model is used as an 'orienting device' and has the opposite effects from those created by applying a 'master' theory or framework. A master framework uses general theory to analyse empirical data in terms of its own frame of reference. Its concepts are either imposed or data are 'fitted into' a pre-established framework of ideas so that research done under its aegis becomes an exercise in self-validation and continual reconfirmation. A master framework thus provides ready-made answers to research questions (and solutions to research problems) and for the most part inhibits the generation of new insights, theory or concepts that challenge its own assumptions and presuppositions.

By contrast, an 'orienting device' is deployed flexibly, simply as a directive for data collection. As such, it also allows for principled co-optation and 'borrowing' from other theories and frameworks. The researcher is encouraged to be curious and to adopt a questioning attitude towards research data. How should these data be interpreted? What is the best explanation for these data? What are the most appropriate concepts? Is this a useful concept? What caused this behaviour? Concepts are not imposed on data or evidence, nor are data forced into pre-existing categories. The approach supports either the flexible generation of new concepts and theory or the modification and refinement of existing ones. While IR cannot *guarantee* conceptual/theoretical innovation, it remains an ever-present possibility and contrasts starkly with the unreflective application or imposition of concepts taken from a master framework.

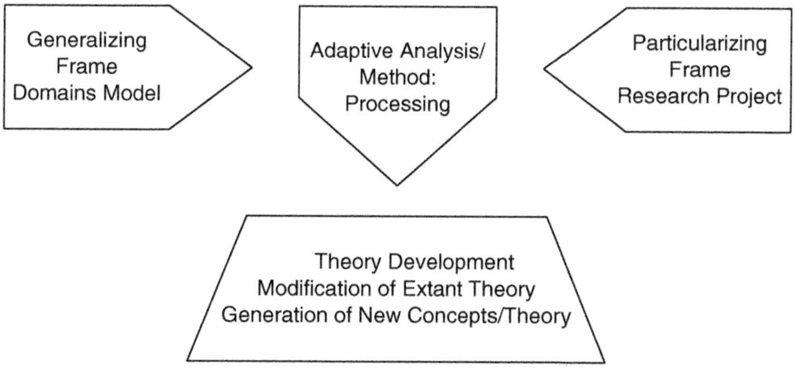

The coupling of the domains framework with a data collecting project – operating according to the principles of adaptive analysis – creates a plastic analytical tool, alive and responsive to novel possibilities of data interpretation. It encourages conceptual, theoretical or explanatory innovation while simultaneously absorbing the insights of 'prior', 'extant' or 'established' theory and concepts. This enables researchers to navigate between interconnected levels and frames of analysis and to explore a greater range of explanatory possibilities. In this sense, a generalizing frame (the domains model) and a particularizing frame (a specific research project-focus) are drawn together through adaptive method and analysis.

Generalizing frame

1. A general model of social reality as entangled, variegated domains.
2. Concepts of power, social relations, subjective experience, interpersonal communication, social organization and asymmetrically distributed resources.
3. 1 and 2 combined, to function as an 'orienting device/framework' for understanding and processing research data.

Particularizing frame

1. A project linking a specific research-focus and problem with techniques and strategies of data sampling, collection and analysis.
2. A focus on a substantive area (for example, health, prisons, probation work, interpersonal relations).
3. Concepts and theory related to the substantive area and research problem (labour markets, doctor–patient relations, professional conduct, careers, mental illness, crime and deviance).

Adaptive method/analysis

1. A method for processing and synthesizing generalizing and particularizing frames.
2. A procedure for developing concepts and theory with regard to a research problem.
3. A multi-strategy method for data collection and analysis focused on the research problem.

Theory develops from research as an effect of the collision and dialogue between generalizing and particularizing frames (see previous figure). The adaptive method synthesizes the complementary insights of the two frames by flexibly linking explanation with description, concepts with data, and theory with evidence. In both frames, concepts are the key to this process, since they allow researchers to understand what the data reveal about social behaviour. As such, concepts inform (sometimes rather indirectly) causal explanations of behaviour as well as research conclusions, such as policy implications. They also shape some practical aspects of data collection by emphasizing particular data collection methods and strategies (including sampling and coding).

As data collection and analysis proceeds, the 'frame' levels and processes work in unison and are reflected in the practical outcomes of research. Depending on their familiarity with IR, researchers will be more or less aware of each element and its role in the overall process. Of course, creativity also depends on flashes of insight, raw intuition or imagination, but to gain more control over the overall process it is best to familiarize oneself with the elements involved in advance. As a general rule, the more unruly flashes of insight, intuition and imagination should be tempered by a modicum of rational steering, in order to more precisely target and understand data.

IR's concern with explanation and causality, with rigorous research strategies and rationales for data sampling, collection and analysis, as well as clear criteria of proof and validity, reflects its embodiment of a set of scientific rules, standards and protocols of method, strategy and analysis. Clearly, this sets IR apart from the view that a 'scientific approach' dehumanizes the social world and social affairs. In sharp contrast, IR endorses a rigorous scientific approach to data sampling, collection and analysis, while simultaneously retaining a view of human beings as knowledgeable and reflexive social agents.

MODIFYING AND CREATING THEORY AND CONCEPTS

The use of concepts from domain theory – or any other conceptual framework – as an initial orientation to data collection and analysis does not stifle the creation of new concepts or theoretical insights. This is because while orienting concepts 'key into' – that is, establish a foothold in – empirical data, they merely *inform* (and are not imposed on) emergent theory and concepts from local data analysis. They are meant merely to stimulate analytical thinking about emerging data. Also, the specific choice of concepts will be influenced by local circumstances and data analysis, including specific problems and research questions. As a consequence, orienting frameworks or concepts remain plastic in relation to ongoing data collection and analysis.

IR allows for a spectrum of *theoretical* responses. On the one hand, these range from the modification, refinement or elaboration of extant concepts and theory, and, on the other hand, to the generation of new (emergent) concepts and theory. However, the ideal position for IR is a combination – an integrated mix – of modification and generation. Also, as far as research outcomes are concerned, the fact that IR accesses both general and local levels of analysis means it incorporates their interweaving influences, thus giving rise to a fairly wide range of typical research outcomes, findings and conclusions. The actual spread of outcomes is depicted in the following table, which shows a sample of research papers which have used domain theory or adaptive analysis (or both) in a more than superficial manner. That is, the authors have drawn upon and utilized them in some depth rather than simply referring to them in passing. Reading from left to right, the first column lists the author and date of publication, the second describes the focus of interest, and the third identifies four types of research outcome, although the boundaries between them are often difficult to draw.

Generic research outcomes

The *first type* (I) (head of third column) features studies directly addressing the domains framework and adaptive theory, either separately or in combination. They are mainly concerned with general issues of theory and methods, while substantive research problems are of secondary concern.

The *second type* (II) features studies that focus on theoretical and substantive issues in equal measure. For instance, Hewege (2010) focuses on management research while also making reference to the agency–structure problem. Hewege and Perera (2013) examine marketing while also assessing adaptive analysis as a method. There is a 50/50 split between generalizing and particularizing themes.

The *third type* (III) is similar to the second in that the discussion of findings and conclusions is also split equally between generalizing and particularizing themes, but with slightly more emphasis on the latter. Thus, many examples strongly feature a substantive area and research an empirical problem, such as motherhood and sport leadership, prisoners' use of in-cell television, police and dyslexia, work/family conflict among female bank workers (in Pakistan), and the adoption of disabled children. These studies have either drawn on a social domains framework to help organize empirical data findings or evidence or they have used an adaptive method for collecting and analysing data. However, the main focus is empirical data/evidence and findings and conclusions based on them.

The *fourth type* (IV) concentrates on single aspects of IR, for example, the deployment of 'orienting' concepts in empirical research (see the health study by MacFarlane and O'Reilly De Brun (2012)). A rather different illustration is provided by Burns (2013), who evaluates the use of typologies as a research tool, in this case in relation to career transitions.

Author and date	Focus	Type of research outcome
Sibeon (2004)	Domain theory and general theory	I
Bottoms (2008)	Adaptive theory/method and criminology	Exclusively general issues
Houston (2010)	Critical realism, action research and social work	
Houston and Mullen-Jensen (2011)	Domain theory and phenomenology	
Carlsson (2004)	Information/management support systems	II
Sealey and Carter (2004)	Domain theory and intercultural communication	Equal split between theoretical and substantive issues [A]
Hewage (2010)	Management and agency–structure problem	
Hewage and Perera (2013)	Marketing and adaptive theory methodology	Explicit reference to general
Van Gramberg (2008)	Meaning, workplace conflict and adaptive theory	Theory and concepts
Candlin (2009)	Professional language and communication	
Leberman and Palmer (2009)	Motherhood, sport leadership and domain theory	III
Knight, C. (2014)	Emotional literacy and criminal justice	Equal split between theoretical and substantive issues [B]
Knight, V. (2016)	Role of in-cell TV in men's prison	
Houston (2015)	Psychosocial domains and social work practice	Implicit reference to general Theory and concepts
Pruulman-Vengerfeldt (2006)	Measuring the information society: Estonia	
Boeck (2011)	Young people and social capital	
Hill (2013)	Police and dyslexia	
Faiz (2015)	Work/family conflict: female Pakistani bank workers	
Bunt (2013)	Adoption of disabled children	
Morris (2011)	Social trust and life insurance	
MacFarlane and O'Reilly De Brun (2012)	Orienting concepts: health research	IV
Burns (2013)	Typologies and career transitions	Particular issues

CUMULATIVE KNOWLEDGE AND THEORY-DEVELOPMENT

All four generic outcomes demonstrate how investigative research feeds into cumulative knowledge as well as theory development. Type I outcomes have an essential role in the more general advancement of social scientific knowledge because explanations of empirical data and evidence require the systematic use of theory and concepts. By contrast, '*ad hoc*' or 'decorative' uses of theory and concepts deal only with 'surface' and presentational elements, and lack explanatory content. Second, genuinely explanatory theory requires some adjudication and evaluation of conceptual materials against empirical evidence or data. In a more empirical direction, some type I research outcomes have very strong connections with social policy issues. For example, in Houston (2010; Houston and Mullen-Jensen 2011), the discussion is around social domains and social work practice, and in Bottoms (2008), the discussion of adaptive theory is with reference to criminological research.

Type II outcomes, with their twin focus on generalizing and particularizing themes and frames, open up links between general theory and empirical or substantive theory, thus linking such research with the wider accumulation of social scientific knowledge. So, for example, social policy implications also result from type II outcomes – for example, about workplace conflict (Van Gramberg 2008) – as well as from type III outcomes – for example, relating to the criminal justice system, as in Victoria Knight's study on the uses and functions of in-cell TV among male prisoners in the UK (2016), or Charlotte Knight's study of emotional literacy, probation officers and their clients (2014).

Both type II and type III research outcomes are at the heart of investigative research since they reinforce and reciprocally feed into each other. Because types II and III partially overlap, they both ensure that practical concerns (of research strategy, methods of data collection, sampling and coding) do not clog up, overwhelm or slow down research projects, at the same time resisting any preoccupation with unduly abstract (theoretical or conceptual) concerns. They represent a balance of

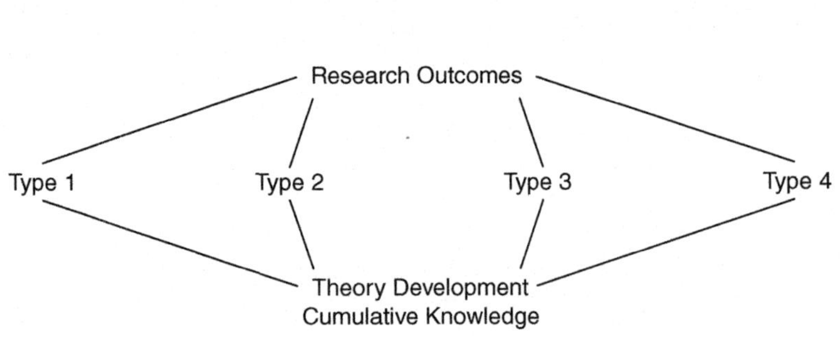

forces in tension between analytical and substantive concerns. Type IV outcomes, which cherry-pick elements or aspects of IR, produce more discrete and incremental, though nonetheless important, contributions to cumulative knowledge.

AN APPROPRIATE MODEL OF SOCIAL REALITY

These considerations about cumulative social scientific knowledge must be understood in relation to underlying assumptions about social reality. IR's capability of generating a broad range of outcomes results from its inclusive model of social reality and its variegated (multidimensional) nature. In relation to this, type I outcomes direct attention to the various ways in which general theory and concepts may be anchored in the empirical world and are pivotal to debates about the nature of social reality. Only an (inclusive) model of social reality can offer the kind of platform that allows constructive dialogue between otherwise competing ontological models. Only such an integrated platform can offer the possibility of rationally based and genuinely cumulative social scientific knowledge. Left to their own devices, 'partial ontologies' (in which one ontological feature or social domain is acknowledged or prioritized) simply undercut and undermine each other's validity claims by excluding (by definitional flat) important aspects of reality. Only within an inclusive ontological framework is it possible to create and sustain a genuinely cumulative growth of knowledge in the social sciences and social analysis.

An inclusive ontology is one in which social reality is understood neither as 'flat', and thus compacted or conflated into a one-dimensional unity, nor is it hierarchically stratified in terms of 'layers' or 'levels' of analysis. Rather, social reality is best understood as multiple, variegated domains which are entangled, enfolded and intertwined in varying empirical circumstances. Only in this manner can an ontological model address the multiplex interrelations of the constituent and irreducible elements of social reality. Partial ontologies can only ever deliver partial knowledge and thus, in themselves, they cannot contribute to the confluence of inputs that are necessary for the cumulative growth of social scientific knowledge.

7

NETWORKS AND DOMAINS: A RESEARCH GUIDE

CHAPTER CONTENTS

In this chapter I discuss some of the practical problems and issues that arise in applying the social domains framework to the design and execution of empirical research. First, because of their relevance to many areas of research, I focus on the nature of 'social settings' and their relation to other domains; in particular, the central pairing of 'settings' and 'situated activity' forms a common motif of many research projects. The discussion attempts to resolve problems in identifying the empirical indicators of social settings. It suggests ways for researchers to search out the most appropriate evidence and forms of data analysis. An important feature of social settings is that they are formed around, and embody, clusters of social networks. Consequently, the discussion mainly centres on the ways in which network settings are shaped by their domain entanglements. The chapter examines research questions about the investigation of networks and their embedding in social domains. The discussion then turns to the value of 'selective focusing' (on domains) and their influence on, and explanation of, social behaviour. This leads to the issue of how domain analysis links up with questions of causality and causal influence in social life. Finally, the chapter considers how the social domains framework helps generate theory from research.

ACTIVITIES AND SETTINGS: A CENTRAL PAIRING

As general features of social reality, social domains are relevant to virtually all empirical areas, topics and problems. This ensures the versatility of the domains model/framework, and thus increases its usefulness as a research tool. As an indication of its potential range of applicability, consider the topics covered in the following empirical studies, which have used core aspects of the IR approach: gate-keeping access to mental health care (McEvoy 2000), female bank workers in Pakistan (Faiz 2015), the adoption of disabled children (Bunt 2013), problems in the training of dyslexic police officers (Hill 2013), prisoners' use of in-cell television (Knight 2016), workplace conflict (Van Gramberg 2008), motherhood and sports leadership (Leberman and Palmer 2009), emotional literacy in the criminal justice system (Knight 2012), gay sadomasochism in the UK in the 1950s (Chaline 2008), young people and social capital (Boeck 2011), professional language and communication (Candlin 2006, 2009), intercultural communication (Sealey and Carter 2004), the information society in Estonia (Pruulmann-Vengerfeldt 2006), leadership of head teachers in primary schools (Archer 2011), management research and marketing (Hewage and Perera 2013), social work practice (Houston and Mullen-Jensen 2011; Houston 2015), and gender and mental health (Bergin et al. 2014).

All these examples highlight the importance of IR's focus on the relationship between social domains and, in particular, the central pairing of situated activities and their typical social settings. In this sense, the diverse research projects above share in common *an attempt to explain observed social behaviour – how and why it occurred – in a particular segment of social life*. Illustrative examples from the list include: how and why probation officers relate to their clients in particular ways (Knight 2014), how and why parents adopt disabled children (Bunt 2013), how head teachers influence leadership in primary schools (Archer 2011), how and why the demands of motherhood impact on sports leadership and vice versa (Leberman and Palmer 2009), and how and why prisoners structure their lives while serving time (Knight 2016).

In terms of domains, explanations of social behaviour centre on a defined pattern of *situated activities* (involving the physical presence of specific people, or their 'absent presence' via emails, telephone and skype, or a mixture of both) played out within *social settings*. Thus, probation officers, McDonald's employees, or hospital personnel operate in very organized types of setting with well-defined boundaries in which 'role expectations' and 'membership rules' significantly affect workers' behaviour. Rules and expectations also play a role for gang members, drug users or even family members, networks of friends and other intimates, although such settings are less bounded and are organized along very different lines – usually more 'informally' and sometimes apparently 'disorganized', at least on the surface.

Thus, the intersection of a specific set of situated activities and their social settings often provides the analytical centre-point and pivot of the research. However, this does not mean that the researcher's attention will always, or exclusively, be on these two domains. The more significant influence of other domains may become apparent as the project unfolds, while the original pairing remains in the background as an important (explanatory) factor. A researcher may be aware of this before the research gets underway as a result of preliminary research or thinking through the implications of the initial problem-focus or research questions. Other domain influences may be noticed as the research proceeds – for example, as when the analysis of newly gathered data or evidence requires a shift in the research focus.

More often than not, the 'time frame' in which such research is set is 'contemporary' or 'present day' (as are many of the examples in the previous list). However, it is also possible to trace changes over lengthier, historical periods of time (as in Chaline's (2008) study of gay sadomasochism in the UK from the 1950s to the present, or my own analysis of the emergence of the acting profession in the UK from the 1570s (Layder 1993). In any case, a present-day focus does not mean that the research is somehow 'detached' from temporal concerns. It is possible to think of contemporary studies as 'snapshots' of events 'frozen in time', but actually, this 'perception' is illusory. In fact, the influences of the domains (and their distinctive forms of power and time) are continuously blending and unfolding in social time–space. More accurately, a 'contemporary' perspective refers to the 'slowing down' (artificially created by the act of analysis itself) of multiple social processes – psychological, interpersonal, organizational and contextual – which are, in fact, continuously unfolding and evolving.

SOCIAL BEHAVIOUR AND SOCIAL REALITY

Many schools of thought and research frameworks have claimed to focus on or 'explain' human behaviour or social interaction, including symbolic interactionism (Mead 1967; Blumer 1969; Becker 1970), ethnomethodology (Garfinkel 1967), existential sociology (Douglas 1977), interaction ritual theory (Collins 2005) and grounded theory (Glaser and Strauss 1967). However, these authors and schools of theory restrict the locus of explanation of social behaviour entirely to its situated dynamics. Other approaches restrict (and thus reduce) the analysis of social reality to a single dimension expressed by such 'unifying' concepts as 'discourses', 'networks', 'figurations' and 'duality of structure'.

For all these authors and approaches, the importance and existence of alternative domains is disputed and dismissed as speculative and/or irrelevant. They claim that social behaviour is to be explained in terms of its constitutive local practices (variously referred to as 'people doing things together', 'joint activity' 'duality of structure', 'participants' main concerns' and 'interaction ritual chains'). Structural or macro phenomena do not 'really exist' (they are inventions of theorists) and thus social reality is fully accounted for in terms of its localized manifestations (of networks, figurations and relational interdependencies). *The only domain or dimension of social life that is of importance is the one in which it is immediately embedded.* So instead of acknowledging the multidimensional (and complex) nature of social life, and that adequate explanation must take this into account, such approaches resort to simplified, reductive models. By contrast, IR calls attention to other (relatively independent but interconnected) domains and social dimensions which are crucial to a rounded explanation of social reality and social behaviour.

DISTINGUISHING SETTINGS FROM LOCATIONS/LOCALES

In gathering and analysing data it is important not to confuse locations, or 'locales', as Giddens (1984) calls them, with social settings. Locales refer to physical aspects of the social environment, such as a street, a shop or a factory, which often simply provide a neutral backdrop to social activities. Although social settings involve physical (architectural) features, they differ from locales in so far as they are organized via networks of social positions, roles, expectations, rules of membership (and supporting discourses), which help to shape social behaviour. Physical locales, by contrast, have less impact on behaviour.

However, during daily and weekly routines, our social activities frequently take place across a number of settings and locales, thus it is important to be able to distinguish between them when interpreting data. Researchers must be confident of being able to say which effects and influences are the result of the setting itself rather than a specific location or locale. In themselves, some locales (streets, offices, city, countryside, houses) are neutral with respect to activity, providing a largely incidental backdrop to it. However, once they are overlain with traces of social organization, such as when a street becomes an arena for gang or turf warfare, or an office or off-site café serves as the focus of a company's employees' interests and activities, then these same locales may sub-serve more important social settings and thus influence the form and content of social behaviour.

PRIMARY AND SECONDARY SETTINGS: TRANSITION ZONES

The researcher must ask him or herself: What is the primary setting of the activity under study? Are secondary settings or locations relevant? Since everyday social activities are embedded in repetitive and cyclical routines (daily, weekly or yearly), then they traverse multiple settings. For instance, with a project on behaviour at work, the influence of the immediate work setting needs to be distinguished from related, transitional zones, as part of the 'enlarged' area of work. For example, if work issues are discussed in a coffee bar frequented by employees, then the physical locale of the coffee bar should be treated as a secondary, but important, setting. This would be the case particularly if a coffee bar or restaurant is actually a part of the workplace (such as in a hospital or on a university campus), rather than a separate, independent business. Such secondary locations create temporary transition zones between phases of work activity and thus play a crucial part in explaining employee behaviour. Alternatively, if a specific coffee bar or restaurant was the focal setting, other locations might then be regarded as 'secondary', such as kitchens or staff rooms serving as 'back stage' areas (Goffman 1967). It should be borne in mind that different sites or locations within a primary setting may, in fact, turn out to be of equal importance.

NETWORKS AND SOCIAL DOMAINS

Networks and social domains are intimately connected in the empirical world. They interweave and intertwine, locking each other into place and creating the fabric of social reality. To speak of 'networks' or 'figurations' as if they were self-sustaining and/or independent of other domains uncouples them from their social anchors and obscures the generative processes and mechanisms which produce them. In this manner, the social world is effectively reduced to a single dimension eliminating a variety of complex influences. As a consequence, relatively autonomous domain processes, such as those involved in self-identity formation, situated activities, settings and contextual resources, are 'lost' to investigation through 'mutual compacting' and 'dissolution', instead of each being treated as important in its own right.

In fact, settings are networks of connections between participants *but they are not simply neutral links in chains of association*. Rather, they are aggregated clusters of social positions, roles, practices and discourses (including those of authority and power) that influence participants' behaviour. However, such network settings vary in the extent of their crystallization – the 'visibility' and density of social bonds, the types of relationship they embody, as well as the clarity of their boundaries with other network settings. Crystallization is directly related to the setting's goals, tasks or purposes, and the manner in which activities are coordinated. They also vary in the 'formality' and the 'explicitness' of their organization and the social principles underlying relationships between participants as well as their legitimacy in the wider social fabric (as in the case of terrorist organizations). Finally, network settings range from highly ordered, organized types to those having a looser, seemingly unorganized character.

Questions for the researcher to ponder are: What does the setting look like? How are its networks organized and what social patterns do their connections make? How does this pattern influence participants' behaviour?

Organized settings and networks

Hospitals or universities, and many work organizations, for example, tend towards the highly crystallized, formal and organized end of the scale. The networks of connections and associations are clear, explicit and ordered. Roles, practices, positions and discourses are highly coordinated and target agreed objectives. The rights, duties and obligations of participants are explicitly defined and follow chains of command, authority, status and responsibility. Sometimes these chains are vertical and hierarchical, while others are 'flat' or 'laterally organized', allowing greater areas of personal autonomy and discretion (see examples below). However, many work and business organizations vary in their outward empirical form and the researcher should be aware of this. Conversely, there are many network settings – such as terrorist organizations – which seemingly lack 'formality' and defined boundaries, but are nonetheless patterned around formal hierarchies of command, power and control (Layder 2004).

Informal settings and networks

At the other end of the scale, gangs, crowds, deviant or marginal groups, musical and artistic groups, and various forms of criminal activity are more loosely organized and coordinated as network settings. Roles, positions and practices (including those of power and authority) are generally not as clearly or formally defined. Nor are there codified (written) rules of conduct specifying members' rights, duties and obligations. The organization or social patterning of such settings is, on the surface at least, 'looser' and more informal than many work and service organizations. Rules of membership, leadership, authority and succession are implicit and chronically 'negotiable' in the form of power plays.

While less ordered and 'formalized', other settings, including families or intimate relationships, are perhaps best thought of as loosely organized, rather than chaotic. While often entangled in deep-rooted and longstanding traditions and values, they are not rigidly defined by any specific 'organizing' authority. As a consequence, people adopt more negotiable and pliable rules, roles and positions. For example, in western culture, friendships and romantic partnerships are constructed and defined in greater measure by the individuals involved rather than by some 'external' authority and/or by the sheer weight of expectation and tradition.

RESEARCH QUESTIONS FOR NETWORKS AND DOMAINS

That networks and social domains are interwoven and connected through social relations of power (over time and space) feeds into research design in the form of an initial problem-focus and some key research questions, as the following examples make clear.

Psychobiographies: research questions

The researcher should seek out data that throw light on the following questions, which identify the psycho-emotional capacities of individuals and explore the extent to which they mesh with network requirements.

1. In what ways do personality characteristics, skills and attributes help or hinder participation in particular networks? For example, fearlessness would be a requirement for a position as a gang leader, while social timidity or shyness would be disadvantageous for professional 'networking'.

2. To what extent do individuals blend in with and/or embrace the ethos and practices of their network? Do particular individuals stand apart or psychologically distance themselves from the network?
3. Do participants' communication skills meet network requirements? Do they display empathy or sensitivity to others, as is required of social workers, psychiatrists and school teachers? Are they driven by selfish or egoistic concerns (as in celebrity and media culture), or are they motivated by community values or altruistic interests (voluntary care work, green protest groups)? How competitive are they (sports men and women, investment bankers, company careerists)? Are specific individuals needy, defensive or passive-aggressive communicators?
4. How do the factors mentioned in 1–3 impact on an individual's relationships and involvement with the network setting? How do individual characteristics shape commitment ('value' or 'continuance' commitment) or attachment to the network settings?
5. What impact do personal qualities have on the focal network setting itself? Do they help to smooth and loosen the flow of information, or do they inhibit and slow it down? Such issues, for example, might be critical factors in some work, management or human resource settings involving divisional or departmental teamwork.
6. Are particular people skilled at switching between (different) networks or within sub-segments of the same one?

Situated activities: research questions

For situated activity, other kinds of research questions grow in importance because there is no clean and separate distinction between the influences of psychobiography and situated activity. Rather, they intermingle and overlap. However, it is important for the researcher to be aware of the distinctiveness of domain influences in order to decide which play a more important role as causal factors in social behaviour. To offer a convincing explanation of a specific set of behaviours, the researcher must find data and evidence that throws light on why and how it occurred. In this sense, some account of causal influence will be invaluable (see later discussion).

1. Is there evidence of participants' interpersonal skills and engagement in productive communication? Communication is 'productive' when it leads to the efficient accomplishment of shared tasks and requires a willingness and ability to cooperate in creative 'synch' with others, despite differences of temperament. (See 3, below.)
2. What styles of interaction and communication are used by specific individuals, teams or sub-groups? Generally, what styles are found in particular settings?

There is a fairly wide spectrum of possible styles, such as 'open', 'engaged', 'business-like', 'guarded', 'officious', 'empathy-based', 'rapport-based' (that is, the use of 'rapport' talk; Tannen 2002).

3. Is there a balance between individual initiative, cooperation and competition between those in regular contact? Such a balance is essential. While the ability to 'get on' and act in concert with other members is important, the smooth operation of a network may be compromised either by too much competition or by too much individuality, initiative and creativity. Either is likely to end in a failure to agree on decisions and objectives. An optimal 'team' or 'network' ethos requires a combination of 'healthy' (but not ego-driven) individuality and 'productive' competitiveness (which encourages innovation).
4. Do participants recognize the distinction between good information (factually based) and good communication (rapport- and empathy-based)? Do they have the skills necessary for both?

Social settings: research questions

1. What is the focal setting (a hospital, a family, a gang, a café, a fast-food restaurant)? What type of setting is it (highly or loosely organized)? How does the organization of the network setting affect the individuals, teams and sub-groups within it? ('Effects' are measured by the quality of communication or group integration, such as the strengthening or deterioration of bonds.)
2. What style of leadership is supported by, and encouraged in, the focal research setting? What other leadership styles are available? Do particular individuals 'take the lead' or 'take the initiative' in setting the agenda? How do situational factors affect behaviour? (For instance, Blanchard (2011) speaks of 'situational leadership'.) Do established (tradition-based) positions and practices interconnect with situational factors? How is this revealed in the data? Answers to such questions will depend on the type of setting. Generally, situational factors influence gang leadership processes (such as competitive power plays or prowess in violence, drug dealing or armed robbery). In professional groupings, leadership positions require defined standards of competence set by professional associations or employing organizations. In 'intimate' settings, influence over others is often established through a shared experiential history and the creation over time of trust, dependence and compassion. The balance between situated and external influences varies markedly in different settings.
3. What features of the setting encourage/support/facilitate the connectivity of the network setting? How does information flow? Does it take the form of 'report talk' (Tannen 2002) in which there is an explicit exchange of facts (details of

meetings, decisions, strategy) mainly concerned with doing or fixing things and accomplishing shared goals and objectives? Or is it in the form of implicit meanings (Bernstein 1973) and meta-messages hidden inside the overt message.

Are participants required to be skilled in both modes of communication? Is there evidence of this? Does the absence or presence of either of these skills impact on network flows? Are there typical sub-groupings of network members?

Contextual resources: research questions

1 In what ways do society-wide divisions such as social class (economic status), ethnicity, gender and age affect the day-to-day operation of the network setting?
2 How are such influences filtered and conditioned by situated activities (social relations and practices) and individual psychobiographies?
3 What is the reach and spread of the focal setting? Is it relatively self-contained (like an office, a company, a house) or is it connected with more encompassing networks (such as global terrorism, mass revolutionary movements, paedophile rings)?
4 How do cultural values, traditions and meanings impinge upon the operation and organization of the network setting? In what ways do they affect its emotional atmosphere/tenor and the contents of communication?
5 Do mass media (and popular or celebrity culture) channel and shape attitudes towards network settings (for example, the importance of particular types of body image or body shape in gyms, and for particular groups such as men and women, and so on)?
6 How do interest groups represent and mould the public profile of settings? For example, think of the comparison between the use of terrorist videos of beheadings and 'legitimate' adverts which co-opt fashion and celebrity culture.

The concerted influence of domains

Without doubt, when considering such questions, a complete and adequate research account will require reference to data drawn from all four domains, since it is their concerted intertwining and reciprocal influences that produce (causally generate) the behaviour in question. This will include some account of the various forms of power and the passage of time (temporality) in the different domains, which has been only partially dealt with here. However, as I shall go on to show, the practical constraints and exigencies of research may mean that the researcher has to concentrate attention on the influence of two or three domains (through selective focusing) in order to highlight certain aspects of a more complex set of causal processes. Selective focusing also allows the researcher to manage the volume of data collected and to make sure that ongoing coding and sampling is kept within manageable limits.

MATCHING CONCEPTS WITH EMPIRICAL INDICATORS

The domains framework offers researchers a set of categories (or conceptual labels) and matches them with descriptive indicators in the empirical world. In effect, it allows researchers to identify empirical evidence or data as representative of particular domains (and their relation to other domains) and greatly helps in classifying or labelling (coding) research data. It does this in an immediate short-term manner, establishing concept-indicator connections as a crucial first step in breaking up (or fragmenting) large blocks of data. This ensures that the research process is easier to manage practically because large amounts of raw (unanalysed) data can create confusion for researchers and thus may block initial data analysis. In addition, fragmenting data simultaneously kick-starts data analysis by furnishing conceptual categories – not only to sort and classify data, but also to suggest more subtle and complex relations between concepts and empirical data. This is necessary in continuously unfolding research with a sharply-focused (but not restrictive) conceptual lens. Thus, continual data analysis is crucial for shaping the forward momentum of the research, including decisions about ongoing sampling issues.

In the longer term, establishing connections between concepts and empirical data is essential to the ongoing 'revision' (or adaptation) of the conceptual framework which guides and shapes the explanatory outcomes of this kind of research. It is an important way of sorting out the influence of causal factors and of tackling why and how questions about the behaviour under the research spotlight. Why are these participants behaving in this manner? What are the consequences of this behaviour for the organization and operation of the setting?

Matching data with domain names reveals connections between different aspects of social behaviour and links them to the combined effects of social domains. However, because of the sheer diversity of circumstances in which they can be found, particular domains may have a wide range of potential empirical indicators. This may cause difficulty for researchers in matching particular examples of data with specific domains. Typically, there are two kinds of problems that may be encountered-selecting data threads, and identifying settings from data.

SELECTING DATA THREADS WITHIN DOMAINS

The first problem concerns making decisions about which of the available data – relevant to a particular domain – is to be regarded as the most pertinent for research purposes. Which strand of data, information or evidence is to be the central point of interest and explanatory relevance? Deciding which data strand(s) to concentrate on within specific domains is usually settled by asking: What are the main problem and topic foci? and What are the 'core' research questions (that give the project its initial impetus)? Settling these allows the researcher to continually refine her or his data search and target data threads (linked segments of data) that clearly reflect the refined problem-focus (and associated core questions). For example, a research project on adopting children has many potential data threads which could be followed up for a particular domain. However, if the problem-focus is on the adoption of *disabled* children rather than children in general, then the relevant empirical threads can be more readily identified (Bunt 2013).

Data threads: adoption of disabled children (Bunt 2013)

Psychobiography: the self of the adopter

Issues around internalizing the role of adopter, such as:

How the adopter's preferences are formed from children's profiles.

The open-mindedness of the adopter as to the scope of impairment of the child.

The felt connection between the adopter and the child (based on film clips and descriptions of the child's personality).

How matches between adopters and children are based on the alignment of their respective tastes.

Situated activity

Interactions and negotiations (meetings and discussions) between: adoption agencies; adopting parents; local authorities; adopting panels.

Focused on issues around:

The scope of the child's impairment and clarity of prognosis.

The adopter's ability to balance compromise with the rejection of children outside their remit.

The setting: the adoption agency

The role of the adoption agency in introducing the child to the adopter.

The agency's need to impart a favourable impression while also being accurate and not disingenuous.

Contextual resources: the macro context

The historical emergence of the culture of adoption practice.

Disabled people considered as 'flawed'.

Subversion of cultural associations with 'normal' life course.

Subversion of idealized notion of childhood.

As this example clearly shows, 'problems' about choosing specific strands of empirical data (facts, information, evidence) *within* particular domains are resolved by asking 'what are the problem- and topic-foci of the research?' This enables the researcher to home-in on specific strands chosen from a potentially very wide range.

IDENTIFYING SETTINGS FROM DATA

The second problem concerns identifying settings from data. While identifying the adoption agency as the relevant social setting in the above example is fairly straightforward, in other cases this may be more difficult. What are a setting's empirical indicators? What kinds of data count as evidence of its existence? Here, empirical variability may make it difficult to identify the basic contours and outlines of a setting, or some sub-segment of it. Such variations are reflected in differences in structure, organization or the setting's wider entanglements with other networks of relationships and spheres of activity. The issue is not resolved simply by checking back to the problem-focus or to the key research questions. Rather, it concerns the kind of empirical data that indicate its overall structure and internal make-up. What is the range of possible forms that social settings may take, and the potential complexity of their internal organization?

The following discussion is meant only to give a flavour of the possible variations in settings that may be encountered. The issues raised may be clarified by asking several related questions. How can we identify the parameters of the focal or primary setting? How can it be distinguished from other settings that are adjacent, interconnected or otherwise entangled with it? How is the setting socially patterned and organized? Which bits or fragments of data relate or belong to which conceptual labels?

VARIATIONS IN ORGANIZED SETTINGS

That formally organized settings are spread across many areas of social life is testament to their many empirical variations in form. Consider, for example, the following: hospitals, schools, universities, churches, benefit/welfare agencies, adoption agencies, local and national/federal government agencies, shops, restaurants, cafés, coffee bars, airports, gyms and leisure clubs, TV and film companies, social work, probation work agencies, the prison service, the police the criminal justice system, the armed forces, and so on. While these are all 'formally organized', there are vast variations in the form they take. Some emphasize hierarchical command structures and top-down flows of communication, while others have flatter, more 'democratic' internal structures.

Work organizations as social settings

Even if we take just one segment of these 'formal' settings, for example, the world of work and employment, the range of empirical variability is marked. This may lead to some confusion in identifying the boundaries between different network settings and between internal and external influences, as well as between different internal elements. In broad terms, work settings vary in terms of their purposive nature. For example, in the *private sector*, work organizations are established to make a profit, by delivering products and services to customers in the marketplace. In the *public sector*, the purpose of organizations is to deliver specific government services designed by politicians or civil servants. In the *voluntary sector*, altruistic aims are more important in driving the design of organizations in order to deliver services to individuals and families (Ashton 2004).

Work organizations also vary in terms of business strategy, division of labour, authority relations, the use of technology, and the distribution of knowledge and rewards. In addition, the type of management style is an important means of controlling the behaviour of subordinates and their motivation to work, and it is crucial to note whether the focus of these relationships 'is on the performance of specific tasks or on the development of their skills' (Ashton 2004: 5). These factors may be combined in different ways to service mass production and/or mass sales or, alternatively, for differentiated production and/or customized selling. Ashton (2004) provides a good example of this by comparing the internal organization of two very different companies; one in the extractive industries, operating along mass production lines, and the other in the chemical industry, delivering innovative products to both the public and other companies. The organizational differences between these companies are summarized below.

Extractive company

Mass production.

Command and control system.

Permanent hierarchy of managers and subordinates (relationships characterized by mistrust).

Delegation of authority and use of external controls and sanctions.

Division of labour: rigid separation between functions and areas of expertise.

Business knowledge and technical expertise restricted to specific groups.

Reward – the result of status.

Chemical company

Innovative products tailored to specific needs.

Minimum hierarchical levels to encourage innovation.

No 'managers'; only 'team leaders', but only for the lifetime of specific projects.

Fluidity of team membership.

Self-managing teams setting own targets, organizing their own work and the delivery of their product or service.

Professional knowledge widely shared (to encourage innovation).

Competitive edge facilitated by spread of information between engineers and others, along informal communication networks.

Team units less than 170 members, to increase effectiveness of communication and operating efficiency.

Relationships of trust and reciprocity between team leaders and team members.

Individual self-monitoring of performance (minimum use of external controls and sanctions).

No institutionalized status differences, no permanent managers and subordinates.

Reward the result of performance (rather than status).

It is clear that the two companies represent differently organized work settings that have very significant effects on workers' behaviour. It is therefore important to be aware of differences within settings when studying or researching work organizations. For instance, identifying how authority and control operates in the chemical company will be harder to pin down in research terms, which will lead to differences in the focus of observations and interviews.

Smaller 'organizations' and informal settings

Some work settings exist on a much smaller scale and (thus) are less organizationally complex than the companies described above. Examples of these are professionals in private practice (such as GPs, dentists, veterinarians, psychologists, psychotherapists and physiologists) or small-scale business ventures (builders, plumbers and electricians). Some work settings in musical, theatrical or entertainment fields are more open, and thus vulnerable to market influences and principles, where careerists move between multiple employers and thus lack the labour market 'shelter' provided by single, 'enveloping' organizations.

In areas that are quite different from work and labour markets, there are less formalized settings, such as those surrounding romantic or couple intimacy, friendship networks, families, street life or criminal gangs. These have a distinctive internal structure but it is less pronounced and defined. The roles and functions of participants, including rights, responsibilities, commitments, attachments, leader and follower relationships as well as the manner in which the 'rewards' of membership are claimed and/or distributed, are much less defined, crystallized and visible. A result of their non-routine, and thus unpredictable nature, is that they tend to blend or merge with the more informal basis leading to arbitrary decisions and interventions by those who wield power and authority.

SELECTIVE FOCUSING

Clearly, all social behaviour occurs within some kind of setting – its immediate social environment – and thus researchers should be aware of the nature of the setting or settings that are the primary focus of research interest. However, this does not necessarily mean that particular domains will be the only or primary focus of the research. Selective focusing is about making research decisions about which domain (or domains) should receive most attention in terms of data sampling, data collection and data analysis. In certain respects, such decisions will be based on pragmatic considerations –in particular, the practical difficulties of maintaining an equally intense focus on all domains (and their variable dimensions of power and time) in the context of a single research project. In most cases this would be too time-consuming, budget-stretching and mind-boggling to achieve in a controlled manner.

Perhaps more importantly, selective focusing directly feeds into the analytical elements, including the analysis of data as they are collected, as well as the development of related concepts. Both are central in IR's attempt to explain the social behaviour under scrutiny. In this regard, attempting to focus on all domains and sub-dimensions within the same project may divert attention from identifying important causal influences. Thus, selective focusing is a means by which researchers can obtain an initial handle on questions concerning why and how particular examples/instances of social behaviour arise – what causes such behaviour? Without some appreciation of the causal influences at work it will be impossible to produce an adequate explanation of the social behaviour in question.

Examples of selective focusing

The above issues can be considered in relation to the Ashton (2004) study mentioned earlier, which highlights how differences in work settings affect the way in which the initial problem-focus is formulated as well as research findings and conclusions.

(a) For example, if the primary research focus was on the ways in which the work experiences of managers or team leaders impact on their personal lives and careers, it would be important to be aware of the influence of internal differences between work settings. A company with a traditional hierarchy, with its delegation of authority, control and sanctions (extractive company), as compared with more fluid, self-managing work teams (the chemical company), will have markedly different effects on individuals' work and career experiences. The primary problem-focus on individual work experiences would mean that the psychobiographical domain would be the main influence on data collection and analysis, while the setting would be of secondary importance. Supplementary data might be gathered on situated activities (interactions with colleagues) and contextual resources (the history of the firm and its competitive relation with others).

(b) Compare this with a project in which the problem-focus is on situated activity. In this case, data are sampled, collected and analysed in relation to activities, interactions and relationships with colleagues, while psychobiographical data (on careers and personal experiences) would be shunted into the background. This might be the case with a project having a social policy or problem-solution orientation (as in action research), in which the objective is to iron out perceived problems within firms or work organizations. The research focus would be on collecting and analysing data (say, from interviews and observations) on typical work practices, networks and forms of communication as a way of tackling and finding solutions for such problems. In this case, data is drawn primarily from the domain of situated activities, but should be balanced, with attention to aspects of the setting (for instance, the more or less fluid or rigid status and reward system). Thus, the setting could be examined with a view to spotlighting a particular problem and the potential ways in which it can be resolved (for example, eliminating inefficient practices or unhelpful and inappropriate modes of communication, or reinvigorating team motivation or group dynamics). In such a case, 'selective focusing' would indicate how situated activities and social settings reciprocally influence each other.

(c) Another problem-focus might centre on the ways in which social settings respond or adjust to changes in external circumstances (contextual resources), such as government legislation, market competition or other economic forces. Of course, such changes are implemented only through human activity, so data on (situated) practices will remain part of the research focus while primary attention will remain on the combined influences of settings and contextual resources.

(d) Yet another problem-focus might be on the historical development of particular firms with a view to examining how factors in (c) (above) have changed over time. Again, psychobiographical elements and situated activities might take a back seat in the research focus and data analysis. However, because historical changes always entail human intervention, there are always secondary implications for these domains.

To summarize, selective focusing on primary, secondary and supplemental domains (including their over-layering effects) reveals causal factors and clarifies the problem-focus by targeting relevant data. This informs the researcher's initial orientation and in turn shapes early data sampling, collection and analysis. Of course, an initial selective focus may be retuned, refined or readjusted as an explanation (or 'theory') of social behaviour begins to emerge from ongoing data collection. Alternatively, while the selective focus may not remain a permanent fixture, it may only be subject to minor revision. The point is that readjustments in 'selective focusing' reflect and indicate the formation of an emergent theory (including concepts and 'explanations' of the focal behaviour). Thus, 'selective focusing', emergent theory and explanation are symbiotically intertwined.

CAUSAL INFLUENCE AND CAUSAL EXPLANATION

While selective focusing provisionally indicates causal influences, a full causal account requires an empirical examination of the specific mechanisms involved. Thus, while selective focusing pinpoints relevant segments of data and is crucial to a full explanation of behaviour, in itself it is not complete. For example, factors such as class, gender and ethnic membership do influence behaviour, even though they are usually but one of a number of influences. Investigative research avoids the over-simplification of single-factor or one-dimensional causality and encourages the researcher to seek more complex multidimensional (heterogeneous) causes of behaviour.

One-dimensional causality: the case of gender and intimacy

Some authors have argued that social behaviour is the result of gender-based differences, especially routine communication and conversational style (Tannen 2002). Thus, it is claimed that communication problems, particularly in the area of intimacy, can be explained by the fact that men and women are locked into conflicting conversational styles, which frequently lead to misunderstandings. Because men and women inhabit 'different worlds' and speak 'different languages', they adopt different communicative styles that affect their ability to understand and to get on (or not get on) with each other. These are summarized below:

Men	**Women**
Directness	Indirectness
Messages	Meta-messages
Report talk	Rapport talk
Information	Connection
Systematizing	Empathizing

They also value and pay attention to different aspects of social life:

Independence	Intimacy/involvement
Competition	Cooperation
Hierarchy/status	Relatedness/connection
Power based on hierarchy	Power based on connection

Such a binary list of behavioural differences creates an over-simplified, and highly stereotyped, view of the relation between gender and human behaviour and creates more confusion than clarity. Understanding social reality as multiple, variegated domains offers a more complex, nuanced view than one in which gender (as an aspect of contextual resources) is thought to be of overriding influence rather than being just one of several domain influences to be taken into account. Thus, factors like gender should not be assumed to be the dominant influence *prior to research investigation*. Rather, research should begin with an open and questioning attitude towards gender influence in relation to a specific research problem. The central questions should be: What is the extent of the influence of gender? What mechanisms produce its effects? How do particular domain influences work themselves out? Such questions alert the researcher to the subtle nuances entailed in a multi-domain account. For instance, varying psychobiographical experiences may have a momentous impact on a person's intimacy, skills and capabilities, or their preferred ways of dealing with emotional issues. Recognizing the effects of individual differences undermines assumptions about stereotypical male or female behaviour.

For example, a preference for using meta-messages in couple relationships – their unspoken, emotional content as compared with spoken, direct messages – is more likely the result of ongoing life experiences than the blunt effects of gender differences. The same applies to empathizing, or being competitive (rather than cooperative) in conversations. These are personal skills which are frequently honed by unique experiences and circumstances, rather than the simple fact of being male or female.

Intimacy and situated activity

The inner dynamics of particular encounters affect participants' behaviour in ways that are specific to those situations. For example, instead of understanding directness as a fixed male predisposition, it is more accurately accounted for as an emergent feature of the ebb and flow of encounters. People are buffeted by rapid changes in the meaning and significance of situations, but respond flexibly as encounters unfold, by reformulating their grasp of events and what they want from them. However, while endeavouring to 'fit-in' with others, uncertainty is produced as participants try to finesse outcomes that personally suit them. The consequent unpredictability of outcomes is further enhanced as those involved adopt novel solutions to problems and ways of responding to others. Given these situation-specific effects, there can be no rigid assumptions about the *overall role* of gender in advance of data collection.

Social settings, gender and intimacy

Furthermore, personal and situation-tied agendas are significantly shaped by social settings. For example, those which have exclusively male or female populations, such as *some* schools, monasteries, nunneries, gangs, prisons or terrorist groups, may attempt a strict imposition of gender-specific behaviour. In fact, this may induce the opposite – of disrupting or re-ordering gender expectations, as in the intense competition and conflict observed in some female gangs (see Cameron 2007). Also, 'informal' areas in some work settings often encourage the subversion of gender stereotypes in which male and female behavioural characteristics vary on a situation-by-situation basis. This is reflected in the deference and compliance displayed by subordinates, irrespective of gender. In such cases, the 'internal' organization of settings enables both men and women to override or modify more generalized gender influences.

Of course, in certain areas, or for specific problems, gender is highly influential in shaping social behaviour. However, only where there is an accumulated body of evidence revealing its exact role can the researcher justify assuming its primary importance prior to research design or data collection. For example, this is the case with domestic violence, male-on-male and male-on-female violence, and serial murder, in which most perpetrators are male, or in depression, where most sufferers are female, and with suicide, in which men far outnumber women. If all that is required is supplemental information to add to such an accumulated body of evidence, then there is some justification for narrowing research attention to a single causal factor, element or variable. But this strategy is inherently limited if the aim is to open up new explanatory ideas, because the most likely result will be to close them down.

Single factors, variables or elements (even domains) are rarely sufficient for an adequate causal account. Their influence develops in concert with others, in a multi-domain world in which mutual interdependence ensures that they are just one of many influences in a complex causal network. IR rests on such assumptions and thus is naturally geared to seeking new angles, perspectives, explanations and novel configurations of causal influence. The model of variegated and entangled domains requires the abandonment of hierarchical, 'top-down' causation (in which social organization shapes behaviour) or 'bottom-up' causation (social behaviour shapes social organization). Also, so-called 'flat' models must be jettisoned because they illicitly reduce social reality to a single modality (such as Garfinkel's 'local practices', Blumer's 'joint activity', Glaser and Strauss's 'structural process' or 'negotiated order', Foucault's 'discourses/power', Latour's 'networks/associations' and Elias's 'figurations/ relational interdependencies'. Flat ontologies de-differentiate social reality and are thus unable to grasp the entanglement of (relatively independent) social domains and their emergent causal outcomes.

RESEARCHING CAUSALITY

There are two distinct types and phases of causal analysis:

- General causal influence (selective focusing).
- Specific mechanisms of causality, or vehicles which 'carry' causal influences.

A combination of both is essential for a complete explanation of social behaviour, and answers the question: How do general and specific factors congeal in particular circumstances?

For example, if a project were to focus on managers' (or team leaders') careers, the relevant domains from which to collect data would be: psychobiographies (individuals' accounts of career experiences) and social settings (the nature of the work organization). Data from these primary domains might be supplemented by data from situated activities (relations and interactions with colleagues) and from contextual resources (the history of the firm and competition with other firms). Framed in this manner, selective focusing sets the scene for a provisional assessment of the causal influence of these domains, which channel and shape data sampling, collection and analysis/interpretation. However, as the research unfolds, this preliminary assessment of 'causal influence' will give way to a search for specific (empirically embedded) causal mechanisms, because a precise account of causality can only be settled through continuous data collection, sampling and analysis (including conceptual development).

Psychobiographical data on managers' or team leaders' career experiences (progress, promotions, blockages, critical junctures) might be compared with data on the nature of the organizational work setting (division of labour, hierarchical versus self-managing groups, career appraisal systems, reward and status structures). Only by sifting, analysing and conceptualizing data in this manner can the researcher accurately judge the strength and balance of the causal influence of settings in relation to psychobiographies and supplementary influences. From this, the researcher might identify specific causal mechanisms and sequences, such as:

> Career appraisal systems —— Division of labour —— chaotic career trajectories —— uncertainty about career progress/outcomes —— conflict with colleagues

By comparison, with a project on couple intimacy, the initial selective focusing might concentrate on psychobiographies, settings and situated activities. To a lesser extent, wider cultural meanings and values around intimacy, romance and emotions (contextual resources) will feed into research considerations. However, the exact details of causal influence can only be determined through ongoing data collection and sampling, for example, from interviews and observations of couples together, and alone, and perhaps through documentary materials (magazines, newspapers, books, videos, film). Analysis of the data might result in the formulation of a causal sequence such as:

> Attitudes towards intimacy (via psychobiographical experiences) —— types of interactional game —— types of intimacy ('episodic' or 'dynamic') —— energizing or de-energizing relationships —— decline or re-stimulation of intimacy

The investigative research approach 'inserts' the researcher into a process of 'pendulation' – a continual oscillation in focus between general causal influences and specific causal mechanisms. This reflects the fact that a full account of causal mechanisms and tendencies can only be disclosed via an unfolding dialogue between emergent theory (explanation), continuous flexible sampling, and the collection and analysis of empirical data.

RESEARCH, CAUSALITY AND THEORY BUILDING

Explanation, causality and theory significantly overlap in meaning. All three address the problem of raising research findings to a level beyond description and classification. Of course, good descriptive skills are essential in social research. However, although necessary, they are merely preparatory steps on the road to explanatory understanding. Explanation confronts 'why', 'what' and 'how' questions, and goes beyond descriptive particulars of concrete sequences of behaviour to ask why they appear at this time and place. What combination of factors and influences produced the behaviour? There is a link with causality here, in so far as the researcher is required to posit causal reasons for the behaviour. What are the empirical mechanisms that produced or generated it? In turn, explanation and causality are also intimately related to theory (and concepts) because theory is a specific type of explanation, one supported by empirical evidence. Another way of approaching this is to say that answers to 'why' questions cannot be simply of the reasoning or logical type; they must be backed-up by empirical data or evidence.

8

CONTINUOUS QUALITY CONTROL

CHAPTER CONTENTS

This chapter outlines and discusses some IR tools which allow researchers to continuously monitor the quality of their research and ensure that checks and balances on quality are always at the forefront of strategic concerns. In this sense, 'quality control' is deeply embedded in IR and the data-gathering projects on which it depends. This chapter expands on some of the themes of Chapter 5, which portrayed a typical IR project as a six-phase cycle in which quality control issues are not restricted to particular phases. For the purposes of this chapter, the six phases can be reduced to three:

Preparatory phase —— Data gathering phase —— Analytical/explanatory phase

The preparatory phase includes: the formulation of research problem(s), topics and questions, the construction of a preliminary explanatory scaffold, a project proposal and a research design.

The data gathering phase includes: typical IR data sampling techniques as well as strategies and methods of data collection (including the IR 'slant' on interviews, observation and documentary sources).

The analytical/explanatory phase includes: the ways in which data are analysed and presented as research findings and/or conclusions, and how the orienting scaffold becomes an 'evolved', 'mature' explanation of the data.

There are two closely-related tools that can be used to monitor quality control. The first is the 'two-tier model' of investigative research, which refers to the coupling of the domains framework with a data-gathering project. The second is the 'IR matrix' or 'research grid', which is a series of practical research dilemmas which map the research area and the researcher's position in relation to it. Both tools are applied to all phases of the investigative cycle. This chapter concentrates on the effects of applying these tools during the three phases identified above and how researchers may use them to ensure consistency of quality in their projects.

QUALITY CONTROL: THE CENTRAL IMPORTANCE OF VALIDITY

In research, quality control refers to the way in which standards or levels of integrity and excellence are maintained. In this sense 'quality control' is pertinent to the quality of the empirical data themselves (quantitative and qualitative, or mixtures of both), as well as the investigative processes, methods and strategies used to collect and analyse such evidence. In Chapter 5, I argued against Tashakkorri and Teddlie (2008), who want to abandon the term, that the concept of validity should be retained as the central indicator of high-quality research – its soundness, robustness and veracity.

Thus, in IR, quality control concerns the validity of research assumptions, premises, processes and findings, including inferences and conclusions. In this sense, validity is closely associated with other related concepts, such as 'plausibility' and 'persuasiveness' (of explanatory arguments and research findings) and 'veracity' or 'truth-content' (of its models of reality, its data, findings, theory/concepts and explanations). Validity is also linked with the terms 'corroboration' and 'verification' (of findings, data or theoretical explanations), and the 'degree of fit' between concepts and evidence. For IR, there are two major aspects of validity – internal and external.

Internal validity points to those 'internal' elements of a research project responsible for ensuring its logical, epistemological and ontological consistency and coherence. Each component or phase must itself be 'internally' consistent and make logical and factual sense, but must also follow on from, and relate to, the other components and phases to form a coherent 'explanatory spine' running through the entire length of the research trajectory. In this sense, findings and conclusions must possess clear logical and factual concordance with initial assumptions, models and premises.

By contrast, external validity refers to the way in which findings and assumptions compare with other research findings, and the extent to which they can be generalized to other cases, areas and circumstances. That is, external validity is relevant to the important question of the generalizability of findings and research strategies. It is also crucially relevant to the issue of the accumulation of social scientific knowledge, which plays a very important role in investigative research. Both generalizability and the cumulative nature of research findings (knowledge) bring into play issues about the potential for the interchange of concepts and theory (Chapter 6), which is an essential feature of IR.

THE RESEARCH PROCESS: A TWO-TIERED MODEL

Typically, research projects rely on a single-tier model in which research questions are investigated via 'appropriate' methods of data collection, which are assumed to be 'neutral' with respect to their implications for research procedures and findings. In this scenario, no deeper questions are asked about the social reality which embeds the research, and general, analytical and theoretical issues are often therefore treated as 'bolt-on' extras, decorative additions, or the result of the routine application – or 'imposition' – of a 'master framework'. Overall, the process is data-centred and data-driven in the sense that specific data or evidence are targeted in advance on the assumption that they will reveal solutions to research problems and questions, and which eventually appear as research findings or conclusions. Consonance between newly gathered data and previous findings will corroborate or verify established knowledge while discrepancies will demand fresh explanations. This process relies on a tight 'internal relation' between local empirical evidence and the application of relevant methods.

Similarly, IR assigns a centrally important role for empirical evidence and the methods and strategies used to collect it. However, the two-tier model – the domains framework coupled with a data gathering project – ensures that the research process is exposed to more general analytical points of reference. The social domains framework connects the empirical project to general theory and analytical issues geared to accessing the complexity of social reality, in particular its variegated (multidimensional) and entangled nature. Thus, it seeks to balance generalizing (analytical) issues with particularizing (local, specific, empirical) influences.

Global (general) and local (specific) properties of social reality

The double-tier model rests on a distinction between global and local properties of social reality. Global features are often overlooked in favour of 'local properties' of social reality (the specific area, data or evidence currently under scrutiny). As a consequence, the tight relationship between global properties and methods and procedures for collecting and analysing data is also under-emphasized. By incorporating the domains framework, IR includes analytical attention to the global (more general) properties of social reality and their 'causal' relationships and influences. Usually such global references are not factored into research designs, or methods and strategies of data collection, and thus have little impact on eventual findings or conclusions. IR endeavours to ensure that both global and local aspects (properties) of social reality are given balanced analytical attention. If local properties – in the form of local data, information, facts and evidence – are given excessive attention, then research becomes myopically data-centred, or data driven. A wider (global) viewpoint can shift analysis away from an exclusive preoccupation with research specifics (targeted information, facts) to include more general considerations about the nature of the reality being researched.

Local properties of social reality are manifest in research data, evidence, facts and information culled from observations, interview transcripts, textual/documentary material, and the like. They can be expressed descriptively and quantitatively, in terms of number, type, incidence, degree, spread, range and distribution, or qualitatively, in terms of 'types' of participants or their lived activities and experiences.

Global properties refer to more general, conceptual and abstract features of social reality and reflect attributes such as complexity and dimensionality, relations and forms of power, temporality and causal mechanisms. Again, these can be expressed 'qualitatively', as in 'career experiences' and 'critical points' (of psychobiography), or the 'elasticity' and 'evanescence' (of situated activity), or as the extent of 'formality' (of social settings). However, they may also be expressed in quantitative terms, such as size, complexity, distribution (of contextual resources), and so on.

Both global and local properties are never *entirely pure in form* since they frequently contain mixes of both elements. However, attention to global properties is minimized, or even excluded, in research which is predominantly data-driven. By contrast, IR treats both global and local properties as equally significant.

THE RESEARCH MATRIX (OR GRID)

The research matrix (see figure below) refers to sets of choices or dilemmas that confront researchers at various points in the research process. IR's two-tier model requires that the researcher constantly attends to these dilemmas, throughout all phases of research – indicated by the term 'pendulation' (see below). The dilemmas are intimately related to quality control since their 'resolution' (or lack thereof) directly affects the overall coherence and persuasiveness of research arguments, and in turn the validity and plausibility of findings/conclusions. The principles and dimensions embodied in the matrix are also those of the two-tier model, which ensures that researchers devote time and attention to balancing and resolving the tensions between dilemmas in their routine research choices. Thus, researchers are immediately and directly engaged with issues of quality control.

The research matrix

Conceptual ——— Empirical
Abstract ——— Concrete
General ——— Specific/Particular
Explanation ——— Description
Theory ——— Reality
Deduction ——— Induction
Objective ——— Subjective

The matrix allows researchers to assess the progress and validity of different aspects of research at it unfolds in real time. For example, it may be used to gauge the extent to which the generalizing and particularizing frames are properly 'meshed' at different phases of a project. The 'grid references' of the matrix 'map' enable researchers to orient themselves in relation to the IR framework as a whole, and to respond sensitively to changing priorities as a project evolves and reconfigures.

Typically, such issues are left implicit and unexamined, or dealt with on a fairly random basis, which unfortunately can lead to distortions of analysis and findings. In contrast, investigative researchers deal with them routinely and systematically and are encouraged to seek a balancing of their effects, thus creating greater coherence and adequacy.

The effects of the two-tier model and the research matrix mean that right from the start researchers find they need to acquire the skills of 'pendulation' – the cognitive ability to move freely 'to and fro' between the extremes of the dilemmas in an effort to achieve an appropriate 'balance' at different junctures of a project. Depending on circumstances, the 'right balance' may actually 'lean towards' one side or the other.

THE PREPARATORY PHASE

Operating in unison in the early phases of an IR project, the two-tier model and the research matrix (or grid) helps researchers to sort out the differences between problems, topics and core research questions. Similar considerations apply to the other preparatory component, the construction of a provisional 'conceptual scaffold', which forms the basis from which a mature explanation of the data will eventually 'evolve'.

Problems, topics and core questions

With IR, it is essential to clearly distinguish between problems, topics and corresponding research questions. In this sense 'research problems' must not be confused with 'practical problems', 'methodological problems' or 'social problems'. IR 'problems' refer to analytical or explanatory issues about the causal influence of social domains on social behaviour. 'Problems' are thus defined in terms of clusters of domain influences giving rise to forms of social behaviour. For example, we may want to explain why there is a high incidence of drug use among certain social groups, say, students (or doctors or professional musicians). The research 'problem' will be to assess which configurations of domain influences (psychobiographies, situated activities, social settings, social backgrounds or 'contextual resources') account for their drug use. Defined in this manner, research problems are primarily, but not wholly, analytical or explanatory in nature, rather than simply practical or methodological. Of course, it is perfectly possible that such analytical problems may well cast light on 'other' kinds of problem. For instance, a causal account of drug use might inform social policy recommendations aimed at 'solving', or ameliorating, the social problem of drug use.

Topics and topic questions

As in the above example, IR's analytical problems run 'in tandem' with the investigation of 'topics', defined as empirical (or substantive) foci of research interest, in this case, drug use among students in college or university settings is the central topic of interest. Topics and topic questions are to a large extent defined in empirical terms, including the types of drug involved, the age groups of users, their social backgrounds (class, ethnicity and gender), and rates of consumption, dependence and addiction. Topic questions appear as factual details, information, incidences, health effects, rates of social withdrawal or exclusion, and so on. The specific times, places and people involved are all important supplementary information. In this sense, 'topics' are expressed primarily as specific, concrete and empirical aspects of social life.

By contrast, 'problems' and 'problem questions' are primarily analytical in that they refer to interconnections between aspects of social reality. They refer to questions about how social domain processes and mechanisms (and their dimensions of power and time) produce particular instances of behaviour. With problem questions, greater emphasis is placed on general, underlying aspects of social reality and social processes. Thus, problems and problem questions tend to be more abstract, conceptual and general (or generalizing) in nature. By contrast, instances of behaviour defined in terms of specific times, places and people are less strongly emphasized.

The parameters set by the two-tier model and the research matrix require that researchers pendulate (oscillate their awareness) between a generalizing frame (enforced by the domains model) and a particularizing frame (the empirical research project). The need to provide a balanced emphasis on problems and topics thus encourages researchers to be constantly aware of the need to fuse their independent but related concerns as data collection and data analysis gathers speed.

Formulating core questions

Defining a problem-focus (and problem questions) allows topic questions to be modified and shaped in order to arrive at the core research questions (Layder 2013). Briefly, this involves three sorts of processes. First, by letting the problem-focus take the lead in defining core research questions, the ever-increasing volume of possible topic questions is curtailed. That is, the potentially infinite number of possible topic questions is reduced to manageable proportions with the questions themselves becoming more streamlined in their analytical relevance. Second, restricting the capacity of topic questions to throw light on analytical issues more sharply targets specific data and empirical areas. Third, the conditioning influence of problem questions on topic questions ensures that empirical (topic) issues never completely hijack research objectives. Particularizing issues of data gathering are constantly conditioned by the generalizing frame of domains. Thus, their mutual relevance and influence are checked against each other, with the effect that the project is never diverted from its explanatory objectives. It never degenerates into a wholly descriptive exercise.

Both the two-tier model and the research matrix reinforce these processes because researchers at all phases of the unfolding research are constantly made aware of the dilemmas between conceptual, abstract and general aspects of analysis as compared with its concrete, empirical and specific elements. In IR, quality control is not the result of separate, punctuated 'injections' at specific junctures, but rather of continual, integral infusions from start to finish. Formulating research questions via the conditioning 'rinse' of a problem-focus ensures that researchers are continually alive to balancing conceptual and empirical emphases in relation to the collection and analysis of data.

CONSTRUCTING A CONCEPTUAL SCAFFOLD

Distinguishing a problem-focus from a set of topic issues frees up the construction of an initial conceptual scaffold which is the analytic basis on which the explanatory spine of the research will rest. At first, the scaffold might consist of only one 'orienting' concept, while subsequently it might include further supporting concepts – either extant or innovative. Over the whole span of the project the mesh of concepts will gradually accrete to form more complex patterns of explanation.

Distinguishing between problem and topic aspects of research questions makes the construction of the initial scaffold a little smoother and easier by ensuring that researchers are sensitive to potential 'quality control' problems. Perhaps the main one is that the conceptual, abstract and generalizing aspects of the scaffold may direct attention away from the concrete, empirical and specific aspects of data. In this respect, the evidential basis of IR – its data, facts and information – must be fully and continuously intertwined with the conceptual and generalizing features of the scaffold. An inherent feature of IR that tends to mitigate the effects of this problem is its phase-cycle form, which only permits the conceptual scaffold to grow and evolve through feedback from ongoing data collection and analysis.

Another quality control aspect of IR is that it distinguishes between types of concepts – 'action/behavioural' concepts, 'system' concepts and 'bridging' concepts – which all correspond to ontological regions/dimensions of the social world. The first two point to what Habermas calls life-world and system sectors, while 'bridging concepts' highlight their intersecting influences (and are specific to the domains framework). This array of concept types sensitizes researchers to data which throw light on the interconnections between different aspects of social reality. Such data point to empirical areas which embed important articulations between the individual and society, agency and structure/system, and the macro and the micro. Thus, the IR approach offers ways in which to map and unpick their empirical and analytical entanglements.

In assembling the conceptual scaffold, researchers benefit by routinely distinguishing between conceptual types, because in so doing their attention is both drawn to the links between segments of reality as well as the empirical data that best 'represents' them. Use of the conceptual types mobilizes awareness of the multiple dimensions of data. It pushes to the fore a sensitive appreciation of aspects of the research process entailed in the dilemmas: general versus specific, conceptual versus empirical, and descriptive as opposed to explanatory. This applies throughout the project, from the initial setting up of the conceptual scaffold, through its development, to its full maturity as an explanation of the research data. As such, awareness of conceptual types leads to continual cross-checking of the validity and quality of data and their analysis. The influence of the conceptual types leaks into, and infuses, succeeding phases, particularly during sampling when different conceptual types may guide the selection of data samples.

THE DATA GATHERING PHASE

IR's default position on data gathering is a multi-strategy approach (Layder 1993). Although it is possible to use IR in conjunction with qualitative or quantitative data in the form of 'mono-methods', it more typically relies on strategic mixtures of types of data and methods in an effort to complement and integrate their effects as well as to enhance explanatory depth and range. For example, IR adds to the quality control criteria of conventional qualitative methods by adding those of the two-tier model. Such 'additions' can be used in tandem and as complementary to more conventional criteria. In this manner, IR's data collection methods and strategies satisfy validity criteria for analytical, general and conceptual aspects on the one hand, and specific, empirical (evidential) elements on the other hand.

These quality control criteria also reshape observation and interviewing in terms of IR's multiple analytical foci. Thus, in IR the emphasis in observation is on maintaining a 'problem-focus', irrespective of the researcher's level of involvement with research participants. That is, 'directed observations' and interviews are defined and guided by problem-foci which are, in turn, shaped by domain influences and entanglements. Problem-focusing gives rise to more refined, empirically detailed 'topic' questions formulated in terms of their 'problem relevance' (see Layder 2013; and Chapter 5). This can be used alongside more conventional notions, such as deploying observation and interviews in close conjunction, so that they continuously cross-check data reliability and validity claims through triangulation. In addition to standard checks on their authenticity, the same considerations apply to the use of documentary sources such as diaries, letters, biographies and autobiographies, newspapers, films and video. IR's default position stresses the use of as many data sources as possible (that is, multiple strategies and methods) in order to strengthen the reliability, adequacy and generalizability of findings.

Quantitative data gathered through surveys often lack analytical or explanatory depth, especially if they are underpinned by a one-dimensional model of social reality. (Pruulmann-Vengerfeldt (2006) has demonstrated how to successfully combine survey data in relation to a domains framework.) However, typically, surveys routinely neglect the social relations, processes and mechanisms which underlie and produce correlations between the 'variables' they study. In addition, survey 'probability samples' are entirely inadequate for investigating experiential and existential aspects of human behaviour (see Chapter 3). The latter require at least some qualitative data or evidence, drawn from 'purposive' samples which, in IR, appear in the form of 'problem sampling' (see below). In general terms, IR relies on a multi-strategy approach in which combinations of qualitative and quantitative data and methods are deployed to investigate integrated features of social reality rather than discrete, isolatable variables.

However, of course, quantitative data produced by surveys frequently provide important information and evidence to supplement or complement qualitative data on the 'experiential core' of social life. In this sense 'concurrent' research designs are the most appropriate since they involve an 'in tandem' mixing and integrating of qualitative and quantitative data. However, the additional use of sequential designs should not be entirely ruled out (see Layder 2013; and Chapter 5). In IR, structured but flexible designs facilitate the 'concurrent' integration of different types of data. In this regard, quantitative data often provide information on the wider macro environment (social settings and contextual resources) which 'enclose' the more micro elements of psychobiography and situated activity. Thus, structured, but adaptive, concurrent designs reflect the manner in which social domains and empirical data reciprocally influence each other.

Flexible concurrent designs also simultaneously support the objectives of explanation and exploration. From an IR point of view, it makes no sense to adopt a 'mixed-methods' separation of 'explanatory' from 'exploratory designs', and treat them as entirely independent of each other (Cresswell et al. 2008; Yin 2009). Instead, exploratory and explanatory aspects should blend and integrate in parallel with the use of quantitative and qualitative data. In this sense, the IR researcher should think in terms of integrated research designs in which segments of data complement and reinforce each other, analytically and empirically creating webs of interconnections between quantitative and qualitative data. Such an overall approach also enhances other aspects of quality control. For instance, domain entanglements become an additional form of 'triangulation' (Denzin 1989). In this respect, multiple domains (reinforced by multiple strategies) require a different but parallel form of cross-checking of data and findings. Specific configurations of domains will be relevant to different research projects driven by particular problem questions. The process of triangulation is an intrinsic part of this in so far as the researcher must select relevant segments of data that reveal the (causal) links between pertinent domains.

Data sampling

Investigative research must always include some qualitative materials/data because probability samples cannot guarantee that a particular problem-focus will be properly represented in such samples. Thus, 'problem sampling' plays a central role in IR. Samples – of interviewees, observations and documents – are selected in accordance with their problem-relevance, and for what they might reveal about the research problem and the core research questions. 'Conceptual sampling' supplements problem sampling by using the conceptual types (mentioned above) to identify data/evidence in support of an emerging conceptual/explanatory scaffold. For instance, the IR researcher may sample around behavioural concepts such as particular 'types' of participant, or around 'system' characteristics such as the social organization of settings. Sampling that is influenced by 'bridging' concepts is able to tackle issues of agency–structure and macro–micro links in social life. Of course, neither 'problem' nor 'conceptual sampling' are meant to entirely displace other types of purposive sampling. Rather, they are intended to take their place alongside others in balanced sampling strategies, which may also include probability samples.

IR's combined theory-testing and theory-generating objectives distance it from what is known as 'theory-based' sampling. For example, problem sampling does not rely on tightly formulated theoretical propositions requiring verification or testing. Rather, a problem-focus and research questions are identified to uncover information which might 'test out' the usefulness of some orienting concepts in the conceptual scaffold. However, problem sampling is, in equal measure, open to the possibility of conceptual (and explanatory) discovery, in the sense of opening up new perspectives on a problem or topic. Thus, IR is guided by the principle that existing concepts and theory should have an equal role alongside conceptual innovation.

THE ANALYTICAL/EXPLANATORY PHASE

In turning to the final phase, it is necessary to reconsider the distinction between 'internal' and 'external' validity. While for IR internal validity primarily concerns issues crucial to the internal coherence and consistency of a research project, it cannot be 'cleanly severed' from external quality control issues. After all, a proper assessment of the validity claims of specific projects can only be achieved by placing them in the wider context of related research, and in terms of how far findings can be generalized to other areas or cases. This is most obviously so with the main findings of a project since they should not be entirely expressed in terms of the data, facts and information. For IR, the emphasis is on producing 'findings' that contain some elements of *explanation* and which allow researchers *to account for* the facts data and information. In some approaches, the data collected during research are regarded almost as their own explanation. In this sense, research questions are answered or resolved by reference to the facts and evidence revealed in data collection.

However, in IR, genuine explanation requires the use of concepts and arguments in the form of explanatory accounts firmly anchored in evidential warrants. In providing such conceptually-based explanations of empirical data, the researcher naturally draws upon and contributes to general issues and themes. In particular, the researcher draws upon cumulative knowledge of the social world – its constituent processes, powers, relations and mechanisms, and how they combine to produce certain effects and consequences. In this sense, the researcher is already engaged with issues of generalizability in relation to the explanatory schema emerging from the current project.

This applies especially to the development of the orienting scaffold as it unfolds and matures throughout the project. In so far as the domains model serves as a general backdrop to an IR project, it injects a level of generality (and links with general theory) which set the terms for the interpretation and analysis of evidence. However, the domains model (and its theoretical assumptions) do not 'predetermine' the explanatory findings of the project because they are only one of a number of formative influences. Other parallel forms of theory and concepts enter the equation and exert independent influences. For instance, the initial conceptual scaffold will consist of at least one (but probably several) orienting concepts, seeding the process by which a mature explanation will eventually evolve. These orienting concepts will be taken from several diverse sources. They may include, for instance, concepts from domain theory, such as the 'duality of social relations', the 'dialectic of separateness and relatedness', domain 'powers' or domain 'entanglements', and so on. However, they may be taken from other general theories, such as Habermas's 'life-world' versus 'system' distinction, or Foucault's 'power and discourse'.

Alternatively, orienting concepts (perhaps drawn from a selective literature review) may be closely linked with an empirical or substantive area such as work, professional behaviour, medicine, deviance, criminality, and so forth. Concepts are chosen, however, mainly for their explanatory, rather than descriptive, value. That is, such concepts should not only indicate or describe an existing state of affairs, but should offer an explanatory insight into *why* this state of affairs exists, or was 'brought into being' in the first place. In this sense, for instance, the concept 'emotional labour' refers not simply to flight attendants' smiles and reassuring behaviour towards airline passengers. It simultaneously points to the connection between the occurrence of such behaviour and employment constraints on workers in public service industries (Hochschild 1983).

None of the concepts finding their way into the cluster forming the initial (provisional) scaffold will predetermine the explanatory findings or outcomes of the project. An IR project is not set up to operate like this. Rather, it has two main objectives: to test/verify elements of the cluster in relation to ongoing data collection and, simultaneously, to seek alternative (new) concepts and theoretical ideas offering stronger, more persuasive explanations of this data. As a consequence, some of the initial orienting concepts may survive relatively intact from their confrontation with incoming evidence, while others will be promoted or demoted in importance. Yet others may be elaborated, reformulated or otherwise 'developed' to achieve greater consonance with the data. Alternatively, innovative concepts and theoretical ideas may develop as the provisional scaffold is forced to jettison its initial explanatory schemas and yield to the formative influence of new data/evidence. In sum, the scaffold evolves organically and dialectically during the unfolding of a project as a consequence of continuous data analysis. At each step of the way the generalizability of the explanatory core of the scaffold is affirmed and expanded in accordance with its plausibility and evidential support.

In addition, references to different levels of social reality, ranging from factual, empirical groundings to more general conceptual elements, are built into final (mature) explanations. Given the continuous fusion of IR's generalizing and particularizing frames, questions about the generalizablity of findings are already, partially, addressed. Of course, this does not entirely resolve questions concerning the typicality or representativeness of data, or indeed the criteria responsible for distinguishing between the research case (phenomenon) and viable alternatives. However, the IR researcher can at least be certain that important aspects of these issues are inherently catered for by the two-tier model.

CONCLUSION

While the elements of quality control discussed above could (correctly) be described as unique to IR, they are designed to sit alongside other established, conventional criteria and modes of quality control to complement, reinforce and integrate their effects. In this manner, they strengthen research validity both in terms of methods and techniques of data collection, as well as in the analysis and explanation of data.

Perhaps the most striking feature of quality control in IR is its continuously integral nature. Quality control is not the application of discrete 'fixes' or 'injections' occurring at specific phases of the research process. Quality control in IR is an ever-present, accretive process in which all its elements are organically interwoven. In so doing they take into account underlying epistemological and ontological issues, which are absent from many, if not most, conventional approaches, while at the same time dealing with practical issues of data collection and analysis.

GLOSSARY OF INVESTIGATIVE RESEARCH TERMS

Action or behavioural concepts

IR distinguishes between three types of concept in terms of their relationship to social ontology – or social reality. Action or behavioural concepts refer to subjective and inter-subjective aspects of social life and are clearly distinguishable from 'system' or 'bridging' concepts (see below). These concepts are pertinent to the domains of psychobiography and situated activity. Examples are those indicating individual attributes and capacities, such as levels of confidence and self-esteem, or of anxiety or security, and so on. They also refer to a person's life-career, their social involvements and relationships over time, and the impact of these on self-identity and subjectivity. Action and behavioural concepts also refer to 'types of actor' or 'participant' (defined either by researchers or fellow participants) as well as to forms of interpersonal control – benign or manipulative (Layder 2004) – or to ways in which people help one another to sustain or maintain identity and meaning in interaction.

Adaptive theory (analysis or method)

An approach to social research (Layder 1998) that emphasizes the combined influence of general theory and evidence-based theory. It has an equal concern with theory-testing (of extant concepts) and theory-generating (developing innovative concepts). Adaptive theory (and method) is intimately linked with the theory of social domains – the 'domains model' or 'framework' (Layder 1997).

Bridging concepts

These concepts refer to social phenomena that 'bridge' the divide between the domains of social reality indicated by 'action' and 'system' concepts. As such, they synthesize radically different features of social reality – its objective, subjective and inter-subjective features. They combine a concern with the psychological involvement of social actors with the social environment of reproduced relations in which they live out their lives. Examples are 'alienation', 'moral involvement' or 'pecuniary involvement', 'commitment' and 'careers'.

Conceptual sampling

Conceptual sampling refers to an IR technique in which decisions about sampling – what to observe, who to interview and which documentary resources to consult – are determined on the basis of their relevance to the conceptual scaffold (see below). Conceptual sampling is an offshoot of 'problem sampling' (see below).

Conceptual (orienting) scaffold

In IR, this refers to the nexus of concepts and theoretical ideas that explain research data. At the beginning of a project the scaffold is provisional and serves as an 'orienting' framework. In later phases, the scaffold becomes firmer as it is reconfigured or confirmed by incoming data. The scaffold eventually forms more complex networks of extant and innovative concepts, both of which are firmly anchored in empirical data.

Contextual resources

This is one of the principal domains underpinning the 'theory of domains' (Layder 1997) and refers to macro-level factors that have society-wide influence on social behaviour. There are two elements: first, distributional inequality between large groupings based on class, gender, ethnicity, age, and so on; second, accumulated cultural resources, such as values, knowledge, fashion, media, and so on. The effects of contextual resources on behaviour are mediated and conditioned by the other domains – psychobiography, situated activity and social settings.

Core research questions

In IR, core research questions are the main driving force of data gathering and so influence the methods, strategies and data analysis. Core questions are composed of a combined selection of 'problem questions' and 'topic questions' (see below), in which problem questions play the most important role.

Directed conversations

Causal or unscheduled conversations can be an important source of information and data. However, in IR such conversations are directed by the researcher so that they are in line with, and reveal information about, the problem-focus and core research questions. To achieve this the researcher must subtly guide informants on to topics that are of most relevance.

Directed interviews

In IR directed interviews have a lot in common with 'in-depth', 'semi-structured' or 'intensive' interviews (Robson 2007; Bryman 2008). The main difference with these is that directed interviews are influenced and shaped by the problem-driven nature of IR and the consequent relevance of the interview questions to the problem-focus and the problem questions that drive the research.

Directed observations

Systematic and structured observation plays an important role in IR. However, the researcher is not constrained in advance of research by a structured schedule defining which behavioural items are to be observed. Observations are systematic and structured in the sense that they are directed in terms of their relevance to the problem-focus and core research questions. As such there is some leeway for researchers to judge which observations and which instances of behaviour are relevant.

Epistemology

A branch of philosophy dealing with the nature of knowledge and with such questions as: How do we know what we claim to know? For research purposes, epistemology focuses on the assumptions that underlie and serve to justify various claims to knowledge. Thus, it is generally concerned with validity, truth, verification and corroboration – the reasons why particular knowledge claims are rejected or accepted.

Investigative research (IR)

This is a summary term that integrates the theory of social domains (particularly its domains model of social reality) and the research principles associated with adaptive theory and method (Layder 1997, 1998).

Master frameworks

IR directly opposes the use of 'master frameworks' which impose preconceived concepts (or whole theoretical frameworks or perspectives) as a way of interpreting and apparently 'explaining' research data – although of course they do no such thing. In fact, imposing preconceived theoretical ideas simply stifles innovation and blocks genuine advances in knowledge. IR operates on the assumption that fresh research data always offers possibilities for reshaping or developing explanatory ideas.

Meta-arguments

A meta-argument is the continuous, overarching argument that runs through the entire explanatory spine of an IR project. Such arguments include initial knowledge assumptions and the model of social reality informing the research as well as data collection and analysis and explanatory findings.

Multi-strategy research

The idea of multi-strategy research was developed in order to maximize coverage of multiple segments (domains) of social reality. It requires the use of as many strategies, methods and techniques of data collection as feasible, practical and necessary in order to create wide and dense data coverage of the empirical focus of a project. The multi-strategy approach is problem-driven in that it attempts to throw light on the problem-focus of the research, rather than to make some some predetermined effort to combine or integrate methods. The emphasis in IR is on the explanatory requirements of a specific problem-focus rather than on mixing methods. The latter tends to make for methods-driven, rather than problem-driven, research.

Ontology

A branch of philosophy traditionally concerned with the nature of social reality as we experience it. However, it refers in a broader sense to what exists more generally, beyond the realm of human experience. In social analysis and research, ontological questions concern the basic nature of society and social life, asking: What is society composed of? What are its constituent elements? In IR, the domains model of social reality is multidimensional and entangled, and as such is aptly suited to researching social complexity. By contrast, one-dimensional models tend to 'contract' and thus over-simplify social reality by reducing it to a single process or principle.

Orienting concepts

These concepts (often chosen from a selective literature review) are used as orienting devices to search out relevant data as well as being a provisional tool for interpretation and analysis. As research proceeds and data accumulate, initial orienting concepts may be reshaped or replaced by others to provide stronger and more persuasive explanations of social behaviour.

Pendulation

In IR pendulation refers to the oscillation in researchers' awareness between crucial dimensions of the research process. This is particularly important in IR were there is equal attention to ongoing data collection (and analysis) as well as to theory development. It is essential at all times that researchers are able to switch the focus between general, abstract and conceptual concerns (theory and explanation) on the one hand and the concrete, specific and empirical aspects of data collection on the other hand. This is essential to quality control and research validity. (See also 'two-tier model of research' and 'research matrix', below.)

Power

In the theory of social domains, power is ontologically plural and varies according to the type of social reality (or domain) from which it emanates. Thus, 'personal' or 'subjective' power is a facet of individual psychobiography, while 'situated' or 'interpersonal power' derives from situated activity. 'Positional' power is a feature of social settings, while 'systemic' (or 'structural') power derives from the domain of contextual resources.

Problem questions (problem-focus)

In IR problem questions derive from a problem-focus since the whole approach is fundamentally problem-driven (rather than methods-driven as in 'mixed methods'). Problem questions tend to be general and analytical in nature and centre on ways in which social domains influence social behaviour. In what ways do psychobiography, situated activity, social settings and contextual resources (and their powers and temporal rhythms) shape social behaviour? Problem questions contrast with topic questions (see below), which are more concrete and empirical and are more focused on data and evidence. Because IR is problem-driven, problem questions have a more important role in the formulation of core research questions.

Problem sampling

In IR 'problem sampling' takes precedence over, but does not completely replace, more conventional forms of sampling. Problem sampling indicates the priority of a problem-focus (and questions related to it) in choosing data samples – the kinds of observations to make, the most relevant people to interview, the most appropriate documents, videos or photographs to scrutinize. However, IR's multi-strategy approach means that 'problem' samples can be, and frequently are, used in conjunction with 'probability' samples (used in surveys). Nevertheless, in IR it remains of overriding importance to select samples based on their 'problem-relevance' since this more accurately indicates the most significant sampling units.

Psychobiography

A principal domain in the theory of social domains, it centres on individual psychobiographical profiles tracing the transformations and alterations in self-identity that result from social involvements and experiences over the lifespan.

Quality control

In IR quality control mainly refers to issues around validity and the validation process in research. Both internal and external aspects of validity are related to the two-tier model (see below), the research matrix (see below), and researchers' skills in pendulation (see above).

Refined interviews

While 'directed' interviews are directed predominantly by the problem-focus and problem-relevance of a project, 'refined' interviews deal with the more specific and local circumstances of the project.

Refined observations

In IR refined observations are more closely guided by the specific and local circumstances of a project. Thus, they are more refined in the sense of being more detailed than 'directed observations', which are shaped more by their relevance to the problem-focus.

Research matrix

Along with the two-tier model of research (see below), the research matrix is a quality control tool that is particularly important for internal and external validity. The matrix itself serves two purposes. First, it is a set of grid references expressed as research (or the researcher's) dilemmas – for example, between an emphasis on either the general or the particular, the conceptual or the empirical, and so on – at particular junctures of a project. Second, it acts as a prompt and reminder for researchers to be continually aware of the need to balance the emphasis in these dilemmas when dealing with data sampling and data collection in order avoid distortions in analysis.

Selective focusing

Ideally, the influence of all domains is important for explaining social behaviour. However, there are very good practical reasons why a researcher cannot focus on all domain influences at once, time, money and energy being three of the most prominent. Selective focusing offers a solution to this problem by restricting attention to one or two domains as an initial focus for data collection and analysis. Focusing can be readjusted as a project unfolds and reveals data indicating the need for such readjustment.

Situated activity

Situated activity is one of the four principal domains in the theory of social domains. It refers to face-to-face (or digitally-mediated) encounters and centres on the meaningful exchanges that occur. It has a dynamic, emergent and evanescent nature, resulting from the arrivals and departures of participants.

Social settings

Social settings are another of the four principal domains of social reality in the theory of social domains. They are the immediate environments of situated activity that are formed through local aggregations of reproduced social relations, positions and practices. Some settings are clearly defined and highly formalized, such as factories, bureaucracies, hospitals and universities, or they can be more amorphous and rather informally organized, as in families, gangs and friendship networks.

System concepts

In one sense, system concepts are the 'opposite' of action or behavioural concepts (see above) in that they refer to (non-acting) patterns of social organization. System concepts refer to social relations that have been reproduced over time through regular, repeated usage. Human actors are constrained by system factors, but also draw upon them as resources that enable them to be creative in their behaviour. In the domains model, system aspects are most in evidence in social settings and contextual resources (including positional power and structural power).

Theory development

IR is 'exploratory' in the wider sense of exploring a problem-focus and the empirical issues around it, rather than in the narrow sense of investigating hitherto uninvestigated topics (although it may do this as well). As a consequence, IR is geared to exploring new concepts and explanatory angles on empirical data and this is reflected in its twin emphasis on theory-testing and theory-generating. The phrase 'theory development' captures the essence of IR in so far as it points to the cumulative advancement of social scientific knowledge. This can only be achieved by utilizing the rich stock of extant concepts and theory (even if they need to be refashioned and/or extended) as well as by consciously seeking out innovative concepts, theories and forms of explanation.

Theory of social domains

The theory of social domains (Layder 1997) offers a multidimensional model of social reality which combines ontological depth and width – as well as all points between. It opposes one-dimensional models, which falsely limit the intrinsic complexity of social reality by reducing it to single unifying principles, such as 'flows', 'liquidities', 'figurations' or 'networks'. The domains model recognizes the variegation of social reality and its constituent processes by qualitatively distinguishing between social domains (and their specific powers and temporalities). Each domain is a discrete segment of social reality, with its own properties and characteristics. Domains are not 'levels of analysis' (such as macro or micro); they are uniquely entangled and configured in varying empirical circumstances. The framework is a 'process model' in which domains link and interlock to produce complex and variable effects on social behaviour. The domains model subsumes both 'depth' and 'flat' ontologies and cannot be reduced to either.

Topic questions

In IR, topic questions primarily focus on concrete and factual data and are filtered and conditioned by problem questions (see above), with their general and conceptual emphases. Problem questions influence and shape the general parameters of topic questions, honing them and sharply targeting them at data that are most relevant to the problem-focus.

Triangulation (of domains)

The domains framework adds to traditional notions of triangulation (based on theory, methods, researchers or data) in that it offers an alternative set of reference points with which to check the validity and accuracy of research findings. The dual nature of the domains framework – a general analytical framework joined with an empirical data-gathering project – adds to its triangulating potential.

Two-tier model of research

IR operates on the basis of a two-tier model of the research process. The first tier is the social domains model (of social reality) with its generalizing frame of reference (including theoretical and conceptual issues). The second tier is the adaptive method, which links it with a particularizing frame – of data collection around a specific research project. IR researchers are required to attend to both frames of reference at all times. Thus, they are able to generate or develop explanations of research data closely in tandem with ongoing data collection. In this sense IR contrasts with many conventional approaches which either rely on a one-tier 'methods and data-driven' model or which treat analytical and empirical aspects as discrete 'injections' at different points in time.

REFERENCES

Archer, A. (2011) *The Role of the Head Teacher in Creating the Cultural Conditions for Distributed Leadership in Four Primary Schools.* PhD, Institute of Education, University of London, UK.

Archer, M. (1995) *Realist Social Theory: The Morphogenetic Approach.* Cambridge: Cambridge University Press.

Ashton, D. (2004) 'The Impact of Organizational Structure and Practices on Learning in the Workplace', *International Journal of Training & Development*, 8(1), 43–53.

Baldwin, L. (2016) *Ice, Ice, Baby? A Sociological Exploration of Social Egg Freezing.* PhD, De Montfort University, Leicester, UK.

Beck, U. and Beck-Gernsheim, E. (1995) *The Normal Chaos of Love.* Cambridge: Polity Press.

Becker, H. (1953) 'Becoming a Marihuana User', *American Journal of Scoiology*, 66, 32–43.

Becker, H. (1963) *Outsiders.* Glencoe, IL: Free Press.

Becker, H. (1970) *Sociological Work: Method and Substance.* Chicago, IL: Aldine.

Becker, H. and Geer, B. (1957) 'Participant Observation and Interviewing: A Comparison', *Human Organization*, 16, 28–32.

Berger, P. and Luckmann, T. (1967) *The Social Construction of Reality.* London: Allen Lane.

Bergin, M., Wells, J. and Owen, S. (2014) 'Gender Awareness, Symptom Expressions and Irish Mental Health', *Journal of Gender Studies*, 25, 141–154.

Bergman, M. (ed.) (2008) *Advances in Mixed Method Research.* London: Sage.

Bernstein, B. (1973) *Class, Codes and Control.* London: Paladin.

Blanchard, K. (2011) *Leadership and the One Minute Manager.* London: Harper Collins.

Blumer, H. (1956, December) 'Sociological Analysis and the Variable', *American Sociological Review*, 21, 683–690.

Blumer, H. (1969) *Symbolic Interactionism.* Upper Saddle River, NJ: Prentice-Hall.

Boeck, T. (2011) *Young People and Social Capital: An Exploration.* PhD, DeMontfort University, Leicester, UK.

Bottoms, A. (2008) 'The Relationship between Theory and Empirical Observations in Criminology', in R.D. King and E. Wincup (eds), *Doing Research on Crime and Justice.* Oxford: Oxford University Press.

Bruyn, S. (1966) *The Human Perspective in Sociology.* Upper Saddle River, NJ: Prentice-Hall.

Bryman, A. (2008) 'Why Do Researchers Integrate/Combine/Mesh/Blend/Mix/Fuse Quantitative and Qualitative Research?', in M. Bergman (ed.), *Advances in Mixed Methods Research*. London: Sage.

Bunt, S. (2013) 'A Framework for the Analysis of the Social Processes in the Adoption of Disabled Children', *Journal of Social Work*, 14(5), 524–541.

Burns, E. (2013) 'Re-Imagining Career Transition: What Help from Typologies', *Journal of Sociology*, 1, 1–17.

Cameron, D. (2007) *The Myth of Mars and Venus: Do Men and Women Really Speak Different Languages?* Oxford: Oxford University Press.

Candlin, C. (2006) 'Accounting for Interdiscursivity: Challenges to Professional Expertise', in M. Gotti and D. Giannoni (eds), *New Trends in Specialized Discourse Analysis*. Berne, Switzerland: Peter Lang.

Candlin, C. (2009) 'Researching Exploration in the Semiotics of Law', in A. Wagner and V. Bhatia (eds), *Diversity and Tolerance in Socio-Legal Contexts: Explorations in the Semiotics of Law*. London: Ashgate.

Carlsson, S. (2004) 'Using Critical realism in IS Research', in E. Whitman and A. Woszczynski (eds), *The Handbook of Information Systems Research*. London: Idea Publishing Group.

Chaline, E. (2008) *From Leather Outlaw to Sexual Consumer? Gay SM in the UK, 1950's to Present*. PhD, London South Bank University, UK.

Charmaz, C. (2006) *Constructing Grounded Theory: A Practical Guide through Qualitative Analysis*. London: Sage.

Charmaz, C. (2008) 'Constructionism and the Grounded Theory Method', in J. Holstein and J. Gubrium (eds), *Handbook of Constructionist Research* (pp. 397–412). New York: Guilford Press.

Charmaz, C. (2012, October) 'The Power and Potential of Grounded Theory', *Medical Sociology Online*, 6(3), 2–15.

Collins, R. (2005) *Interaction Ritual Chains*. Princeton, NJ: Princeton University Press.

Cresswell, J. (1998) *Qualitative Inquiry and Research Design: Choosing among Five Traditions*. London: Sage.

Cresswell, J. (2009) *Research Design: Qualitative, Quantitative and Mixed Methods Approaches*. London: Sage.

Cresswell, J., Plano Clark, V. and Garret, A. (2008) 'Methodological Issues in Conducting Mixed Methods Research Designs', in M. Bergman (ed.), *Advances in Mixed Methods Research*. London: Sage.

Denzin, N. (1989) *The Research Act* (3rd edition). Upper Saddle River, NJ: Prentice-Hall.

Dey, I. (1999) *Grounding Grounded Theory*. San Diego: Academic Press.

Douglas, J. (1977) *Existential Sociology*. Cambridge: Cambridge University Press.

Dunning, E. and Hughes, J. (2013) *Norbert Elias and Modern Sociology*. London: Bloomsbury.

Durkheim, E. (1952) *Suicide: A Study in Sociology*. London: Routledge.

Etzioni, A. (1961) *The Comparative Analysis of Complex Organization*. New York: Free Press.

Faiz, R. (2015) *Work–Family Conflict: A Case Study of Women in Pakistani Banks*. PhD, University of Hertfordshire, Hatfield, UK.

Foucault, M. (1970) *Discipline and Punish: The Birth of the Prison*. Harmondsworth: Penguin.

Foucault, M. (1980) *Power/Knowledge: Selected Interviews and Other Writings 1972–1977*. Edited by C. Gordon. Brighton: Harvester.

Garfinkel, H. (1967) *Studies in Ethnomethodology*. Upper Saddle River, NJ: Prentice-Hall.

Geertz, C. (1973) *The Interpretation of Cultures: Selected Essays*. New York: Basic Books.

Giallombardo, R. (1966) 'Social Roles in a Prison for Women', *Social Problems*, 13, 268–288.

Giddens, A. (1984) *The Constitution of Society*. Cambridge: Polity Press.

Giddens, A. (1987) *Social Theory and Modern Sociology*. Stanford, CA: Stanford University Press.

Giddens, A. (1992) *The Transformation of Intimacy*. Cambridge: Polity Press.

Glaser, B. (2001) *The Grounded Theory Perspective: Conceptualization Contrasted with Description*. Mill Valley, CA: Sociology Press.

Glaser, B. and Strauss, A. (1967) *The Discovery of Grounded Theory*. Chicago, IL: Aldine.

Goffman, E. (1967) *Interaction Ritual*. New York: Anchor.

Goffman, E. (1983) 'The Interaction Order', *American Sociological Review*, 48, 1–17.

Goldthorpe, D. (2000) *On Sociology: Numbers Narrative and the Integration of Research and Theory*. Oxford: Oxford University Press.

Habermas, J. (1986) *The Theory of Communicative Action. Vol. 1: Reason and the Rationalization of Society*. Cambridge: Polity Press.

Habermas, J. (1988) *The Theory of Communicative Action. Vol. 2: The Critique of Functionalist Reason*. Cambridge: Polity Press.

Hammersely, M. and Atkinson, P. (1983) *Ethnography: Principles in Practice*. New York: Tavistock.

Hearn, H. and Stoll, P. (1975) 'Continuance Commitment in Low-Status Occupations', *Sociological Quarterly*, 16, 105–114.

Hewage, C. (2010) 'Resolving the Structure-Agency Dichotomy in Management Research: the Case for Adaptive Theory Research Methodology', *Proceedings of 24th Annual Australian and New Zealand Academy of Management Conference*, 8–10 December, Adelade, South Australia.

Hewage, C. and Perera, L. (2013) 'In Search of Alternative Methods in Marketing: Insights from Layder's Adaptive Theory Methodology', *Contemporary Management Research*, 9(3), 343–360.

Hilbert, R. (1990) 'Ethnomethodology and the Micro-Macro Order', *American Sociological Review*, 55, 794–808.

Hill, A. (2013) *Policing Dyslexia: An Examination of the Experiences and Perceptions of Dyslexic Police Officers*. PhD, De Montfort University, Leicester, UK.

Hochschild, A. (1983) *The Managed Heart*. Berkeley, CA: University of California Press.

Houston, S. (2010) 'Prising Open the Black Box: Critical Realism, Action Research and Social Work', *Qualitative Social Work*, 9(1), 73–91.

Houston, S. (2015) 'Enabling Others in Social Work: Reflexivity and the Theory of Social Domains', *Critical and Radical Social Work*, 3(2), 245–260.

Houston, S. and Mullen-Jensen, C. (2011, June) 'Towards Depth and Width in Qualitative Social Work: Aligning Phenomenological Analysis with the Theory of Social Domains', *Qualitative Social Work*, 10, 266–281.

Knight, C. (2014) *Emotional Literacy in Criminal Justice: Professional Practice with Offenders*. Basingstoke: Palgrave Macmillan.

Knight, V. (2012) *A Study of In-Cell Television in a Closed Adult Male Prison: Governing Souls with In-Cell Television*. PhD, De Montfort University, Leicester, UK.

Knight, V. (2016) *Remote Control: Television in Prison*. Basingstoke: Palgrave Macmillan.

Knight, V. and Layder, D. (2016) 'Concept-Formation, Complexity and Social Domains: Investigating Emotion(s) in a Prison Setting', *Sociological Research Online*, 21(4), 5.

Layder, D. (1985) 'Power, Structure and Agency', *Journal for the Theory of Social Behaviour*, 15(2), 131–149.

Layder, D. (1990) *The Realist Image in Social Science*. London: Macmillan.

Layder, D. (1993) *New Strategies in Social Research*. Cambridge: Polity Press.

Layder, D. (1997) *Modern Social Theory: Key Debates and New Directions*. London: University College London Press/Taylor and Francis.

Layder, D. (1998) *Sociological Practice: Linking Theory and Social Research*. London: Sage.

Layder, D. (2004) *Emotion in Social Life: The Lost Heart of Society*. London: Sage.

Layder, D. (2006) *Understanding Social Theory* (2nd edition). London: Sage.

Layder, D. (2009) *Intimacy and Power: The Dynamics of Personal Relationships in Modern Society*. Basingstoke: Palgrave Macmillan.

Layder, D. (2013) *Doing Excellent Small-Scale Research*. London: Sage.

Leberman, S. and Palmer, F. (2009) 'Motherhood, Sport Leadership and Domain Theory: Experiences from New Zealand', *Journal of Sport Management*, 23, 305–334.

Luckenbill, D. (1979) 'Power: A Conceptual Framework', *Symbolic Interaction*, 2, 97–114.

Lull, J. (1990) *Inside Family Viewing: Ethnographic Research on Television Audiences*. London: Routledge.

MacFarlane, A. and O'Reilly De Brun, M. (2012) 'Using a Theory-Driven Conceptual Framework in Qualitative Health Research', *Qualitative Health*, 22(5), 602–618.

Malone, M. (1997) *Worlds of Talk*. Cambridge: Polity Press

Marshall, A. (2006) *I Love You but I'm Not in Love with You*. London: Bloomsbury.

Marx, K. and Engels, F. (1968) *Selected Works*. London: Lawrence & Wishart.

McEvoy, P. (2000) 'Gatekeeping Access to Services at the Primary/Secondary Care Interface', *Journal of Psychiatric and Mental Health Nursing*, 7, 241–247.

Mead, G. (1967) *Mind Self and Society*. Chicago, IL: Chicago University Press.

Merton, R. (1968) *Social Theory and Social Structure*. New York: Free Press.

Miles, N. and Huberman, A. (1994) *Qualitative Data Analysis: A Source Book of New Methods*. Thousand Oaks, CA: Sage.

Miller, M. (1995) *Intimate Terrorism: The Crisis of Love in an Age of Disillusion*. New York: W.W. Norton.

Mills, C. (1940) 'Situated Actions and Vocabularies of Motive' *American Sociological Review*, 5, 904–913.

Moores, S. (1993) *Interpreting Audiences: The Ethnography of Media Consumption*. London: Sage.

Morris, L. (2011) *Social Trust and Life Insurance: The Impact of Genetic Test Results in the Republic of Ireland*. Newcastle upon Tyne: Cambridge Scholars Publishing.

Nye, J. (2011) *The Future of Power*. New York: Public Affairs

Parsons, T. (1951) *The Social System*. London: Routledge.

Patton, M. (2001) *Qualitative Research and Evaluation Methods* (3rd edition). Thousand Oaks, CA: Sage.

Polsky, N. (1967) *Hustlers, Beats and Others*. Chicago, IL: Aldine.

Pruulman-Vengerfeldt, P. (2006) 'Exploring Social Theory as a Framework for Social and Cultural Measurements of the Information Society', *The Information Society*, 22, 1–18.

Punch, K.I. (2008) *Introduction to Social Research* (2nd edition). London: Sage.

Reibstein, J. (1997) *Love Life: How to Make Your Relationships Work*. London: Fourth Estate.

Riemen, D. (1986) 'The Essential Structure of a Caring Interaction: Doing Phenomenology', in P. Munhall and C. Oiler (eds), *Nursing Research: A Qualitative Perspective* (pp. 85–105). Norwalk, CT: Appleton-Century-Crofts.

Ritzer, G. (2011) *The McDonaldization of Society* (6th edition). Thousand Oaks, CA: Pine Forge Press.

Robson, C. (2007) *How to Do a Research Project*. Oxford: Blackwell.

Rock, P. (1979) *The Making of Symbolic Interactionism*. London: Macmillan.

Rorty, R. (1979) *Philosophy and the Mirror of Nature*. Oxford: Blackwell.

Rose, N. (1991) *Governing the Soul: The Shaping of the Private Self*. London: Routledge.

Shutz, A. (1972) *The Phenomenology of the Social World*. London: Heinemann.

Sealey, A. and Carter, B. (2004) *Applied Linguistics as Social Science*. London/New York: Continuum.

Searle, J. (1998) *The Mystery of Consciousness*. London: Granta Books.

Sibeon, R. (2004) *Rethinking Social Theory*. London: Sage.

Spenser, L. and Pahl, R. (2006) *Rethinking Friendship: Hidden Solidarities Today*. Princeton, NJ: Princeton University Press.

Stebbins, R. (1970) 'Career: The Subjective Approach', *Sociological Quarterly*, 11, 32–42.

Strauss, A. (1987) *Qualitative Analysis for Social Scientists*. Cambridge: Cambridge University Press

Strauss, A. and Corbin, J. (1990) *Basics of Qualitative Research: Grounded Theory Procedures and Techniques*. Newbury Park, CA: Sage.

Sykes, G. (1999) *The Society of Captives: A Study of a Maximum Security Prison*. Princeton, NJ: Princeton University Press.

Talisse, R. and Aikin, S. (2008) *Pragmatism: A Guide for the Perplexed*. London: Continuum.

Tannen, D. (2002) *I Only Say This Because I Love You*. London: Virago.

Tashakkori, A. and Teddlie, C. (2008) 'Quality of Inferences in Mixed Methods Research: Calling for an Integrative Framework', in M. Berman (ed.), *Advances in Mixed Methods Research*. London: Sage.

Van Gramberg, B. (2008) 'Investing Meaning in the Workplace: The Potential of Adaptive Theory', *Journal of Science, Technology and Management*, 1(1), 69–78.

Yin, R. (2009) *Case Study Research: Design and Methods* (4th edition). London: Sage.

Yin, R. and Davis, D. (2007) 'Adding New Dimensions to Case Study Evaluations: The Case of Evaluating Comprehensive Reforms', in G. Jules and D. Rog (eds), *Informing Federal Policies for Evaluation Methodology*. San Francisco, CA: Jossey-Bass.

INDEX

Note: Tables and Figures are indicated by page numbers in bold print.